A LITERARY REVIEW

SØREN AABYE KIERKEGAARD was born in Copenhagen in 1813, the youngest of seven children. His mother, his sisters and two of his brothers all died before he reached his twenty-first birthday. Kierkegaard's childhood was an isolated and unhappy one, clouded by the religious fervour of his father. He was educated at the School of Civic Virtue and went on to enter the university, where he read theology but also studied the liberal arts and science. In all, he spent seven years as a student, gaining a reputation both for his academic brilliance and for his extravagant social life. Towards the end of his university career he started to criticize the Christianity upheld by his father and to look for a new set of values. In 1841 he broke off his engagement to Regine Olsen and devoted himself to his writing. During the next ten years he produced a flood of discourses and no fewer than twelve major philosophical essays, many of them written under *noms de plume*. Notable are *Either/Or* (1843), *Repetition* (1843), *Fear and Trembling* (1843), *Philosophical Fragments* (1844), *The Concept of Anxiety* (1844), *Stages on Life's Way* (1845), *Concluding Unscientific Postscript* (1846) and *The Sickness unto Death* (1849). By the end of his life Kierkegaard had become an object of public ridicule and scorn, partly because of a feud that he had provoked in 1846 with the satirical Danish weekly *The Corsair*, partly because of his attacks on the Danish State Church. Few mourned his death in November 1855, but during the early twentieth century his work enjoyed increasing acclaim and he has done much to inspire both modern Protestant theology and existentialism. Today Kierkegaard is attracting increasing attention from philosophers and writers 'inside' and outside the postmodern tradition.

ALASTAIR HANNAY was born to Scottish parents in Plymouth, Devon, in 1932 and educated at the Edinburgh Academy, the University of Edinburgh and University College London. In 1961 he became a resident of Norway, where he is now Emeritus Professor of Philosophy at the University of Oslo. A Fellow of the Royal Society of Edinburgh, he has been a frequent visiting professor at the University of California, at San Diego and at Berkeley. Alastair Hannay has also translated Kierkegaard's *Fear and Trembling*, *The Sickness unto Death*, *Either/Or* and *Papers and*

Journals for Penguin Classics. His other publications include *Mental Images – A Defence*, *Kierkegaard* (*Arguments of the Philosophers*), *Human Consciousness* and *Kierkegaard: A Biography*, as well as articles on diverse themes in philosophical collections and journals. He is the editor of *Inquiry*.

A Literary Review

Two Ages, a novel by the author of
A Story of Everyday Life, published by
J. L. Heiberg, Copenhagen, Reitzel, 1845

REVIEWED BY
S. KIERKEGAARD

Translated with an Introduction and Notes by
ALASTAIR HANNAY

PENGUIN BOOKS

PENGUIN BOOKS

Published by the Penguin Group
Penguin Books Ltd, 27 Wrights Lane, London W8 5TZ, England
Penguin Putnam Inc., 375 Hudson Street, New York, New York 10014, USA
Penguin Books Australia Ltd, Ringwood, Victoria, Australia
Penguin Books Canada Ltd, 10 Alcorn Avenue, Toronto, Ontario, Canada M4V 3B2
Penguin Books India (P) Ltd, 11, Community Centre, Panchsheel Park, New Delhi – 110 017, India
Penguin Books (NZ) Ltd, Private Bag 102902, NSMC, Auckland, New Zealand
Penguin Books (South Africa) (Pty) Ltd, 5 Watkins Street, Denver Ext 4, Johannesburg 2094, South Africa

Penguin Books Ltd, Registered Offices: Harmondsworth, Middlesex, England

First published 1846
This translation first published 2001

2

Copyright © Alastair Hannay, 2001
All rights reserved

The moral right of the translator has been asserted

Set in 10/12.5 pt Postscript Monotype Bembo
Typeset by Rowland Phototypesetting Ltd, Bury St Edmunds, Suffolk
Printed in England by Clays Ltd, St Ives plc

CONTENTS

A Literary Review

I would like to dedicate my translation to
HUBERT L. DREYFUS

TRANSLATOR'S INTRODUCTION

The name Kierkegaard is mostly associated with works by which the Danish author was best known in his lifetime, first and foremost *Either/Or* but also other such oddly memorable titles as *Fear and Trembling*, *The Concept of Dread*, *Philosophical Fragments*, *Concluding Unscientific Postscript* and *The Sickness unto Death*. What we easily forget is that these and other works appeared under pseudonyms. Why Kierkegaard resorted to pseudonymity is the subject of much speculation, but he himself provided one quite plausible explanation. In a short work, *The Point of View for My Activity as an Author*, published after his death, he says in effect that the pseudonymity was designed to let the works express views of life without the reader being led to think they might be the actual views of the author. His own task as a writer Kierkegaard took to be that of promoting in individual readers a sense, first, of a need for such life-views and, second, of the ways in which certain prevalent life-views, the kind he called 'aesthetic', were inadequate to the individual's true needs. The task, as he saw it, was to begin with the inadequate views and convey somehow the ways in which they were deficient. More generally, his project was aimed at the cultivation in the reader of what one pseudonymous author in particular, Johannes Climacus, calls 'inwardness' (*Inderlighed*). This is not, as the English word suggests, a self-centred absorption in the states of one's own mind or soul, but an engagement by the whole person in life's tasks.

It need come as no surprise, then, to those who know Kierkegaard only through his pseudonyms, to find how sharp an eye the poet-philosopher of inwardness has for the ways in which people fail to engage themselves in this way. More surprising, perhaps, is the skill with which, in *A Literary Review*, he relates such failure on the part of the individual to features of society and cultural life at large. The work includes one of the most startling pieces of cultural analysis to be found anywhere.

A Literary Review was published in Copenhagen on 30 March 1846. Kierkegaard had begun writing it while waiting for proofs of the work with which he intended to mark the end of his pseudonymous authorship, the aptly named *Concluding Unscientific Postscript*. That authorship, of a series of works starting with *Either/Or*, had occupied him for four intensive years during which he also wrote a series of signed works described as 'edifying' and 'Christian' discourses. The sequence of events which turned Søren Aabye Kierkegaard (the surname an earlier spelling of the Danish for 'graveyard', *Kirkegård*) to full-time authorship began in 1837 when he met Regine Olsen, daughter of a Copenhagen dignitary. Regine was then fourteen years old. Their later engagement and his breaking it off were to provide the focus of much of his writing. The following year Kierkegaard's father, Michael Pedersen Kierkegaard, died, aged eighty-one (Søren was then twenty-five). The death led Kierkegaard, after ten years as a student, finally to complete his university exams and face the future.

Kierkegaard was born in Copenhagen on 5 May 1813. His father's family had worked the land of their local pastor in East Jutland, in a feudal arrangement that gave the family its name. Kierkegaard's father himself had been released from formal vassalage at the age of twenty-one, at a time when he had already moved to Copenhagen to work in an uncle's hosiery business. He later became a wealthy wholesaler of imported goods, and Søren inherited a fair fortune when his father died. Søren was the youngest of seven children whose mother was their father's second wife, and who had formerly been maid to the first. A brother and a sister died before he was nine. His two surviving sisters, a brother and his mother were all dead by the time he was twenty-one, and Søren, now alone with his father and his eldest brother, himself became convinced he would not live to be more than thirty-three. He was educated at the prestigious Borgerdydskole (School of Civic Virtue), where he gained a reputation for a quick tongue and a sharp wit, and then at the University of Copenhagen, where he enrolled in 1830. His chosen subject was theology, but he also studied liberal arts and science, excelling in the latter, and spent in all ten years as a student, his father, until his death, footing the not inconsiderable bills.

Just one month after Michael Pedersen Kierkegaard died, Kierkegaard published his first book, *From the Papers of One Still Living*, though the title derives not from his father's death but from that of his teacher and mentor, Paul Martin Møller (1794–1838). A little over two years later, on 10 September 1840, he became engaged to Regine and began work on his doctoral dissertation. He also underwent the necessary practical training for a career in the State Church and gave his first sermon. However, almost immediately after his successful defence of his dissertation ('On the Concept of Irony with Constant Reference to Socrates') on 29 September 1841, Kierkegaard broke off his engagement to Regine, and by November the break was final and he was on his way to Berlin on the first of four visits he would make to that city. These, apart from a day trip to Sweden, were the only journeys he made outside Denmark. Ostensibly for the purpose of attending Friedrich Schelling's widely advertised lectures Kierkegaard also devoted much of his time on this first Berlin visit to writing a large part of what was to become *Either/Or*.

The reasons for his break with Regine are much disputed. The crux, however, seems to have been Kierkegaard's sense of his inability to express or – to use a term from *Either/Or* – 'reveal' himself in terms of civic virtue, or 'ethics', in a sense that gives a central place to civic responsibility and the maintenance of traditional institutions such as marriage. Although the parts of *Either/Or* that he was writing in Berlin were a defence of marriage ('Or'), the case for it was posed in opposition to a diversely represented 'aesthetic' view of life ('Either'). The reader is thereby faced with a choice in which the real author's preference, if any, can play no part, concealed as the author's true identity is under a barrage of pseudonyms.

The two-volume *Either/Or*, also edited by a pseudonym, 'Victor Eremita', was published in February 1843, to be followed in October by two slimmer volumes, *Repetition* by 'Constantin Constantius' and *Fear and Trembling* by 'Johannes de silentio'. The first of these hints at a religious view of life, which the latter then illustrates in a rather startling way with the story of Abraham's willingness to sacrifice Isaac, his son, indicating that faith has nothing to do either with reason or with 'ethics' in the sense just mentioned. All three works deal with the problem of entering society in the way such an ethics prescribes, what the pseudonymous authors call 'realizing the universal [or general]'. This same theme was to be pursued in the substantial *Stages on Life's Way* edited by Hilarius Bogbinder, published in April 1845. But already in June 1844 there had appeared two pseudonymous books introducing new topics, *Philosophical Fragments* by Johannes Climacus and *The Concept of Dread* (or Anxiety) by Vigilius Haufniensis. The former sought, in subtle and spare language, to suggest an alternative way of grasping essential truth to that proposed by philosophy, a theme to be resumed and reworked in the much larger *Concluding Unscientific Postscript to the Philosophical Fragments*, and published under the same pseudonym early in 1846. *The Concept of Dread* examined the psychological background to the experience of sin, at the same time implying a radical critique of contemporary theology.

The manuscript of *Concluding Unscientific Postscript* was delivered to the printer at the end of December 1845 and published on 27 February 1846. Ten days later, on 9 March, Kierkegaard wrote a lengthy 'Report'. It includes the following remark:

Concluding Postscript is out; responsibility for the pseudonyms acknowledged; one of these days the printing of the *Literary Review* will begin. Everything is in order; all I have to do now is keep calm and say nothing, relying on *The Corsair* to support the whole enterprise negatively, just as I want it.[1]

We shall return to *The Corsair*, a radical and somewhat scurrilous weekly, in a moment. Kierkegaard adds:

My idea is now to qualify for the priesthood. For several months I have prayed to God to help me further, for it has long been clear to me that I ought not to continue as an author, which is something I want to be totally or not at all. That's also why I haven't begun anything new while doing the proof-reading, except for the little review of *Two Ages* which is, once more, concluding.[2]

The not so little review translated here, a signed work published three weeks later, seems to have been intended as the first of a revived genre in Kierkegaard's authorship. Though in fact no further examples appeared (the only previous one was his first publication, *From the Papers of One Still Living,* ostensibly a review of Hans Christian Andersen's *Only a Fiddler (Kun en Spillemand)*), the review format now appealed to him for a special reason not unconnected with his thoughts about abandoning a writer's career:

To now I have served by helping the pseudonyms become authors. What if I decided from now to do what little writing I can indulge in in the form of criticism, putting what I had to say in reviews which developed my thoughts out of some book or other? So they could also be found in the book. Then at least I'd avoid being an author.[3]

Having his own thoughts look as though they emerged from the work of another author would relieve him of the inconvenience of inventing new pseudonyms for them. As the opening quotation above mentions, Kierkegaard had already declared (in an unpaginated final section of *Postscript*) that his was the pen behind the pseudonyms. Of course everyone in the closely knit world of Copenhagen letters knew this, but according to the manners of the time they would not say so publicly until the real author owned up.

The declaration added to *Postscript* was partly forced upon Kierkegaard by certain events involving *The Corsair,* events which caused him to delay delivering its final text until the very last moment.

I was momentarily in two minds as to whether, in consideration of the circumstances (the *Corsair* nonsense and town gossip), to leave out the acknowledgement of my authorship and just indicate that the whole thing was older than all this babble by giving the dates in the printed material. But, no! I owe it to the truth to ignore this kind of thing and do everything as decided, leaving the outcome to God's will and accepting everything from his hand as a good and perfect gift, scorning to act from prudence, putting my hopes in his giving me a firm and wise spirit.[4]

Although the *Corsair* affair began under cover of pseudonymity, it quickly became personal. Under the pseudonym Frater Taciturnus (from *Stages on Life's Way*), Kierkegaard had provoked the periodical to attack him (under that pseudonym) by disclosing the identity of one of its anonymous authors. The author in question, Peder Ludvig Møller (1814–65), a writer, poet and literary critic with academic ambitions, wished his connection with *The Corsair* to remain a secret for fear of spoiling his prospects for a professorship in aesthetics at the University. Earlier Møller had criticized the work of Frater Taciturnus. Knowing of the connection, Kierkegaard made it public in a newspaper article published on 27 December ('An Itinerant Aesthetician's Activity and How He Nevertheless Came to Pay for the Banquet'), in a breach of etiquette that was also a morally mischievous act.

In its 2 January issue *The Corsair* responded in kind. It attacked Kierkegaard, not as Frater Taciturnus but in person, with accompanying caricatures of his crabwise gait, stoop, thin legs and apparently uneven trouser legs, and cane or umbrella in hand. *The Corsair*'s coverage in the months that followed made Kierkegaard a household name and fair game for the mockery of the town's youth. The streets in which he was already a well known figure became places of constant harassment.

Yet, as both the first and the last passages quoted above indicate, this is something Kierkegaard seemed actually to want, and after all it was he who provoked the response. Although he may not have expected such a direct reaction, it seems clear that it was in this way that he thought his enterprise could be 'supported negatively', as the first quotation has it. Some explanation of this strange idea will be found in the later pages of this translation with their talk of the 'unrecognizables' and of 'suffering action', pages which he was very likely penning while the *Corsair* affair was upon him.

Drafts for the *Review* had already been written shortly after the novel reviewed first appeared. The novel itself, *Two Ages* (*To Tidsaldre*), had been published in October 1845 and was the latest from the hand of Thomasine Gyllembourg, an energetic and talented writer who made her literary debut at the exceptionally late age of fifty-three.

Before the turn of the century Thomasine Christine Buntzen, daughter of a bourgeois Copenhagen family, had married the radical poet P. A. Heiberg, twenty years her senior. He was exiled in 1799 for political activities, and on forming her attachment to the man who became her second husband, Carl Frederick Ehrensvärd, Count Gyllembourg, a wealthy Swede who was also a political exile, Thomasine divorced Heiberg. Out of resentment Heiberg made his nine-year-old son, Johan Ludvig, a ward of court, though later relented. After her second husband died in 1815, Thomasine moved in with her son who was already establishing a name for himself as a writer. These two, later joined by the leading lady of the Danish stage, the half-German actress Johanne Luise Pätges, whom Johan Ludvig Heiberg married in 1831 when he was approaching forty, enriched Danish cultural life with a much sought-after salon whose welcome the young Søren at one time eagerly solicited. Madame Gyllembourg herself was able, with her own talent and the help of her entrepreneurially as well as artistically gifted son, to establish a reputation as both a significant writer and a pioneer of modern Danish prose fiction, writing under the signature 'The author of *A Story of Everyday Life*' (in exactly the same way that her contemporary, Walter Scott, signed his works, the so-called Waverley Novels, 'The author of *Waverley*').

Originally, *A Story of Everyday Life* was a feuilleton in the manner of Balzac, published serially in *Kjøbenhavns flyvende Post* (Copenhagen's *Flying Post*, referred to usually just as *Flyveposten*), her son's literary journal. At one time badly needing to fill space in that paper, Heiberg had asked his mother for help. She provided it, on 12 January 1827, in the form of a fictitious letter to the editor which caused a considerable stir not least among those curious to know who the writer was. She wrote more, the letters then taking on the form of instalments in a developing story later published, in 1834, in collection, as *The Family Polonius*.

Two Ages, which was to be Madame Gyllembourg's last work, tells the story of a family whose fortunes span the immediate post-revolutionary age, the age of honour, loyalty and passion, and the advent of a rational and reflective modernity, the present age, an age of calculation and prudent choices. Given her own connections and Denmark's place in Napoleonic politics – when her serviceable merchant fleet came under the eyes of both Britain and France, Denmark had sided with the latter – the author's familiarity with both ages enabled her to portray them in miniature in the local setting of Copenhagen. The age of revolution is reflected in the youth and love story of Claudine, who falls for a young Frenchman, Charles Lusard, a member of the French legation newly installed in Copenhagen. Claudine's loyalty to the memory of Lusard, who has left to join the army, is rewarded after many vicissitudes by a reunion when she discovers that he has been living in an inherited estate in Jutland in the firm belief that she, Claudine, was married and living in Germany. The focus of the story reflecting the later age, 'the present age', is the return to Copenhagen in 1844, after a long period abroad in both Europe and America, of their now fifty-year-old son, also called Charles. What he finds, as Kierkegaard puts it in his résumé in the *Review*, is a Copenhagen without legations or any other intimations of 'world-historical denouments' in the offing, but a life

undisturbed by the energetic passion whose form is in its very energy – yes, even in its vehemence – and isn't hiding the power of a secret and forbidden passion. On the contrary, everything is manifestly nondescript, and thus trivial, formless, knowing, coquettish, and openly so. Here there is no great revelation and no deep secret, but superficiality all the more. (p. 24)

This Lusard, living alone with his recollections, seeks a worthy heir, someone close whom he can make happy, and the story ends in a form of 'repetition' in which another faithful woman is eventually reunited with her lover.

Repetition, as his introduction shows, is a leitmotif for Kierkegaard's own interest in the work. Preceded, typically, by a preface saying that his review is written only for those with the time and patience to read a little book – though even they needn't bother, and those 'whose critical and aesthetic education comes from reading newspapers' are excused altogether – Kierkegaard's Introduction reminds 'the author of *A Story of Everyday Life*' of an earlier reference to 'his' work ('his' in order to respect the formality and ignorance as to the author's identity) in his own first publication, *From the Papers of One Still Living*. The *Review* is thus given the appearance of being the fulfilment of a promise Kierkegaard had earlier made to himself to return to this author at a later date. At the end of a lengthy appreciation, he hopes the author will find him

unchanged or, if possible, changed in the repetition: a little more clarity in presentation, a slightly lighter and more flowing style, in recognition of the difficulty of the task a little less hurried, a little more inwardness in the discernment: in other words, changed in the repetition. (p. 20)

Incidentally, the anonymous author's son, Johan Ludvig Heiberg, had found Kierkegaard's manuscript of the earlier treatment of his mother's work stylistically deficient and, whether for that reason or not, had not given it room in his journal. Moreover, Heiberg had made uncomprehending remarks about one of Kierkegaard's pseudonymous publications, precisely *Repetition*, not grasping that 'repetition' meant a kind of inner revision of the motivation with which one approaches the same life-situations. Not one quick to forget a personal injury, Kierkegaard was without doubt addressing Heiberg here as much as the latter's mother, and putting him straight on the subject of repetition. Also, in praising Madame Gyllembourg (though never by name) for even-handedness in her treatment of the two ages, and allowing his résumé to conclude with Lusard's 'Amen' to a declaration of faith in human progress, Kierkegaard is preparing the way for a far more pessimistic account of the present age, a view more in keeping with the gist of his pseudonymous works to which his own *Postscript*, the work he was still completing when Madame Gyllembourg's book appeared, had just been added.

For reasons explained in the *Review*, neither of the reunions that end each part of the novel (or each age) is a 'repetition' in the proper sense introduced in his pseudonymous book of that name. Nor is the reunion that ends the second part properly a repetition of the one that ends the first. Instead of being the product of a resolute will to risk everything, it is formed in the light merely of recollection. The second Lusard, after his long travels now no longer young, having 'let the time of love pass by, having turned off at the point where a person's future really begins, has beautifully installed himself in remembrance and chosen the past, wanting only to secure a memory for himself in making one member of his family happy' (p. 24).

What Kierkegaard especially prizes in the novel is the author's ability to portray the ties of family life as a medium in which the larger currents of the life of the times are reflected. The author herself puts it very neatly in her Preface:

The subject I have wanted to treat is not the great events that so violently shook the close of the previous century and still agitate our present day, not the reflected image in our fatherland of that raging storm, nor the cold misty air it left behind, but only what I would call the domestic reflection [*Reflex*] of it, the effect it has had in family life, in the personal relations, in the ideas and views of individuals, an influence that has consciously or unconsciously touched everyone.[5]

In the last recognizably reviewing part of *A Literary Review*, the section called 'An Aesthetic Reading of the Novel and its Details' giving portraits of the leading figures from each age, Kierkegaard points out that the author does not intend these to be mere personifications of the age. Rather they are persons whose *fates* bear the character of the age, and are largely determined by the broad outlooks distinguishing the two ages. Rather than in the psychology of the parties involved, these outlooks are reflected in the stories themselves, their settings and outcomes.

In the long final section entitled 'The Results of Observing the Two Ages', Kierkegaard offers an extended analysis of the present age, preceded by a much shorter account of the age of revolution. Towards the end there is an apocalyptic crescendo in which the reader is told that a movement is afoot, called 'levelling', which, driven by the abstract notion of 'the public', in turn the creation of the press, will end inexorably in a state of culture where individuals lose their identities and will, for the first time as single selves, confront the choice between nothing and God.

For the author of *Postscript*, a work commonly regarded as devastatingly critical of Hegel, the language of this final section may sound surprisingly Hegelian. There is talk of an Idea. For Hegel, the Speculative Idea was an ideal of unified understanding which can be seen to be working itself out in history. But this way of talking was prevalent at the time even among those who rejected Hegel and his 'speculative' idealism. As many did in his time, Kierkegaard uses 'Idea' to refer to the sort of goals that motivated the revolutionary age. Chief among these are freedom and equality. The reader of the *Review* will find in what Kierkegaard has to say about 'levelling' a radical revision of the ways in which equality was generally understood, namely in terms of what, for Kierkegaard, are merely external factors. Typically, Kierkegaard believes that ideals of any kind are centred in the individual and not in a developing cultural environment. Any Idea, then (but let us just say 'idea'), should have the form of an 'inner drive' that 'propels the individual on'. These expressions come towards the end of a passage concerning what it really means to act from principle. As usually understood, to act from principle means to apply some rule that one has inherited, learned, internalized or in some way subscribes to. But in what Kierkegaard takes to be its proper sense, a 'principle' is what 'comes first', and that for him is 'the substantial, the idea in the unopened form of feeling and enthusiasm' (p. 90).

A formless society, such as the one Kierkegaard in his résumé of *Two Ages* describes the later Lusard as finding on his return from his travels, is one in which the 'passionate' distinction between form and content has been 'annulled'. Loss of form does not mean shapelessness or chaos or madness; it means loss of enthusiasm. For Kierkegaard form is a visible feature of the individual's life due to the sincerity and focus that belong to enthusiastic activity on behalf of an ideal. The less the pursuit of ideals originates in individual enthusiasm, the less essential becomes the truth of the ideal thus fulfilled. In a common manner of speaking, we might say that acting 'ideally' in that way would be 'merely' a matter of form, a formalism, while in its proper sense form, for Kierkegaard, is a matter of the individual's wholehearted engagements. Essential meaning and content, whatever might seem their 'inadequate limitation', must be due to a 'self-deepening' (p. 90).

There can be sheer enthusiasm; it is the idea in its substantial but, as Kierkegaard says here, unopened form. In the age of revolution the idea unfolded, but it did not open fully. It was only a *kind* of opening, a partial revelation as well as a revolution, but still only half-way – indeed, an expression of human immaturity. Kierkegaard refers here to the 'reactionary immediacy' (p. 57) reflected in the domestic life portrayed in Part One of *Two Ages*, the part devoted to the age of revolution. Rather than being self-determined, the actions of the persons involved are reactions to events, and they lack constancy for that very reason. Substituting a favourite astrophysical analogy for the botanical one, Kierkegaard says that 'the harmony of the spheres' is the unity of every planet relating to itself and to the whole. Take one of these relations away and you get chaos. But in the human case the idea is an additional factor to take into account: 'Remove the relation to oneself, and we have the mass's tumultuous relating to an idea; but remove this too [i.e. the relating to the idea], and we have rawness [*Raahed*]' (p. 55).

At the bottom of the scale, then, we encounter raw and unformed behaviour, the behaviour of the mob. Because it lacks a centre of gravity, or indeed any internal structure at all, the mob is at the mercy of suggestion and governed by primitively holistic psychological reactions. But a group or crowd can also be inspired by a revolutionary ideal. It then acquires a structure even though its members are still not separated out singly as enthusing individually for the ideals inspiring the revolution. There is indeed passion, in contrast to a cold formalism, but it is due to the mutual encouragement of numbers and can result in the violence of a Reign of Terror. What is needed is the individual's own relation to the idea.

The remainder of the *Review* focuses on this relationship of the individual to an ideal, in order to arrive at an account of an age that, even if it does not comprehensively contradict Lusard's 'Amen', at least leads us to suppose that, if its ideals are to be achieved, something far deeper than the resources provided by the author of *Two Ages* will be required.

Typical of an age such as the one that Lusard meets on his return to Copenhagen is a 'crippling and disheartened, tactless, levelling reciprocity' (pp. 55–6). Kierkegaard takes 'levelling' to be the nemesis of his age, a catastrophe blocking off what appears to be the only viable path to human completion. But if carried to extremes, it is also able – and here we have a hint of what Kierkegaard's 'negative' enterprise might concern itself with – to produce a crisis that reawakens individuals to other possibilities. The metaphor of levelling has many applications. Most historical examples are, in a very literal way, down to earth: agrarian agitators tearing down hedges enclosing common ground, or park palings as well as hedges in the case of Crown lands. These physical levellings were, of course, in the service of a political ideal that can be called levelling, but in a more abstract way. In his first reference to levelling in the *Review*, Kierkegaard speaks of it in what seems to be an even more abstract sense. He describes it as a 'quiet, mathematically abstract affair', one that 'avoids all fuss [*Ophævelse*]' (pp. 74–5). This in itself suggests that Kierkegaard is not talking politics.

Kierkegaard's criticism of *Two Ages*, tactfully elicited more in what he is able to extrapolate from the novel in his own terms – those of the pseudonymous authorship – than in what he says directly against it, is that *its* 'totality', the life-view that defines the frame of the novel's main characters' responses, is not ethical but aesthetic. He notes the aesthetic limitations of the viewpoints of the characters, the women in particular. Claudine, whose story provides the main thread of Part One, faced with the disappearance of her loved one to the wars and with looking after herself and her child, sees her own situation in an openly romantic light, constant in her love for Lusard but with a fixed picture of herself and Lusard that allows no inward development. The corresponding figure in Part Two, Mariane, with no illusions and made to work as a servant, develops a 'quiet inwardness' in the face of the humiliations to which she is subjected. But in so far as it fails to reveal itself in the visible forms required of ethics, even quiet inwardness is still an aesthetic state. If ethics is to find its place in the world, Mariane's tenuous foothold on the 'singling out' that the proper unfolding of the idea requires would need encouragement in the age at large. But it is precisely this further development that the levelling process prevents. It is a process of spiritual stultification, and were it not for the fact, as Kierkegaard sees it, that it has reached a point where its own momentum will carry it to its logical conclusion, levelling might even look like a deliberate attempt to escape the spiritual discomfort of being a singled-out individual, a self with no identity in group-membership terms, whether of a nation, an estate, an association or whatever other form of collectivity.

Shunning the singled-out state even receives ideological support in what Kierkegaard refers to here as 'the idolized positive principle of sociality'.

[This] in our time is the consuming, demoralizing principle, which in the thraldom of reflection transforms even virtues into *vitia splendida*.[6] And to what can this be due other than to a disregard for the singling out of the religious individual before God in the responsibility of eternity? When terror begins here, one seeks comfort in company, and reflection then captures the individual for life. And those who didn't even notice this crisis beginning fall without further ado under the relation of reflection. (p. 76)

So levelling is not deliberate in any literal sense. No one actually chooses this stultifying path and, as if on an escalator going down instead of up, everyone is in any case to some extent on it. What is entirely negative about levelling is, in brief, that it is set on eradicating the unique locus of human fulfilment, the human will, the only place where the ideal can arise in the way it must, in the form of sustained concern on the part of the individual. In a reflective age the proper flowering of the idea in the individual has been brought to a stop by an externalizing of its goals. The way in which politicians aim to introduce equality is one in which, as Kierkegaard says in a passage deleted from the final draft of the *Review*, 'the dialectic turns away from inwardness and wants to render equality in the negative; so that those who are not essentially individuals constitute an equality in external association'. Levelling, he adds, is 'the faked anticipation of eternal life, which people have done away with as a "beyond" and now want to realize here *in abstracto*'.[7]

The criticism clearly embraces not just politics but the whole of culture, that is to say, the ways people interrelate at all levels. In the *Review* Kierkegaard identifies the psychological attitude corresponding to levelling as 'envy'. In an entry in his journals he calls it a 'self-establishing envy' in which, in order to advance in one's own esteem, 'one wants to drag down the great'. But so deeply embedded is this envy in the collective consciousness, or so far in the background, that nobody sees it for what it is. Superiority in others is treated as hubris on their part, but the very fact of admitting their superiority betrays an underlying envy or resentment.[8]

We note that Kierkegaard says 'one' wants to drag down the great. The use of the term 'one' (*Man*, as in the German from which Heidegger coins the notion of *das Man*) implies an anonymity. It is not you or me that wants to drag a superior person down, but rather, you or I do it because *one* wants to do so. If you were to look for someone responsible for levelling, worse than there being no one at home when you knocked on the door there would be no door to knock on. What has levelled (in the transitive sense) in such a case is 'the public' (p. 84). Kierkegaard says the public is levelling's 'spirit', a 'monstrous abstraction, an all-encompassing something that is nothing, a mirage . . . [a] phantom' (p. 80). More particularly it is a phantom brought about by the press.

Although the remarks about 'one' wanting to drag down the great bear the heading, '*The Corsair*'s Standpoint', these words about an abstraction are addressed not to *The Corsair*, which with its radical stance could hardly claim to represent Copenhagen's journalistic establishment in any case, but to journalism in general and the liberal press in particular.

Still, in Kierkegaard's eyes, that periodical was certainly an instrument of the levelling he writes about in the *Review* and whose spirit was the public. Moreover, an allegory that he uses to illustrate the sinister side of levelling, with its seat in the anonymous public, anticipates his own fate at the hands of *The Corsair* so closely that it may have been inserted at the last moment when those events had actually begun to unroll, making the streets of Copenhagen uninhabitable for him. We must recall, however, that Kierkegaard regarded this not as fate but as something he had brought upon himself deliberately.

Kierkegaard's long subsection on 'the present age' returns in conclusion to those features of Copenhagen life in 1844 noted by Lusard on *his* return: triviality, formlessness, a 'know-it-all' attitude, flirtatiousness and superficiality. Enlarging on this list, Kierkegaard asks: What is it to chat? What is formlessness? What is flirtatiousness? What is superficiality? What is it to reason? In each case the answer is some variation on the theme that the 'passionate' distinction between inner and outer, between the intensive and extensive, has been done away with. The features in question all represent a 'suspension of the principle of contradiction', the consequence of which is to place the existing individual in 'contradiction with himself'.

As hinted earlier, towards the end of the long 'Results' section of the *Review*, analysing the two ages, Kierkegaard assigns a role to 'the unrecognizables [*de Ukjendelige*]' (p. 96). These are people who have grasped that the 'meaning' of levelling is its ability to expose individuals to a fundamental choice: nihilism or service on behalf of God. The task of the unrecognizables, quite unlike that of the recognizable leaders and role models of the past, will be to help others towards this insight. They must do so without imposing themselves on those others as authorities on the subject, since that would detract from the fundamental nature of the choice in those in whose service they work. It would also imply that they themselves were somehow absolved from choosing.

Having brought his account of the present age to its apocalyptic conclusion, Kierkegaard signs off in his usual manner with a playful disclaimer. He hasn't tried, he says, any more than the author of *Two Ages*, to judge or compare the merits of the ages portrayed – all he has done is describe them. This is a little disingenuous, since he has approached the events described in the book from another and higher point of view. That in itself, quite apart from being a kind of judgement on *Two Ages*, implies a radical corrective to the optimism shown in its author's 'even-handed' treatment of the respective merits of the two ages it portrays.

Kierkegaard ends, however, by being even-handed himself, with a Hegelian twist that to a Hegelian would nevertheless appear quite unHegelian. He asks the reader to balance the advantages of the present age's 'extensity' against the 'intensity' it is increasingly losing, and offers, in the name of Socrates, a third alternative: first, the spontaneity of an immediate inspiration (as in the age of revolution); second, the growth of understanding and ingenuity in the service of prudence (a proper use of reflection, the present age's typical mode); and third, the highest and most intensive inspiration of a Socrates who sees very well what the prudent thing to do is and then does not do it (p. 99).

The suggestion is, in any obvious sense, outrageous as a rule for the maintenance of life, but perhaps less so as a proposal about how to grasp the character of life as seen from some point of view beyond purely utilitarian considerations. Did Kierkegaard see himself as writing in the 'cause' of such a proposal, or perhaps just from the point of view of such a perspective? Did he really think such a proposal might be able, through the medium of politics, to affect the very manner of life's maintenance, the sociopolitical structure, replacing its inherent utilitarianism for instance? Or was the Socratic image merely a fanciful projection of his own 'outsider's' position vis-à-vis the circles on which he hoped his writings would have some impact?

All this remains unclear. The same is true of how far the apocalyptic vision of a purely levelled world was for him a genuine fear. If it was, did he regard his remarks in 'Results' as prophecy? If so, were he alive today would he see his prognosis realized in *our* present age? If yes, should we regard him as truly a prophet? What in fact would confirm such fears, genuine or not? Marxism, modern nihilism, drug addiction, fashion, spectator sports, the Internet?

Kierkegaard, we recall, it having long been clear to him that he 'ought not to continue as an author', had decided not to begin on anything new while reading the proofs of *Postscript* 'except for the little review of *Two Ages* which is, once more, concluding'. But by the beginning of the next year he was dismissing plans to give up writing as a lapse of nerve. Also, it might look as if *The Corsair* had forced him to stop. In 1847 he published *Edifying Discourses in a Different Spirit* (probably misleadingly rendered as 'in Different Spirits') and the substantial *Works of Love*, regarded by some as his greatest work. In the spring of 1848 there followed *Christian Discourses*, and in 1849 *The Lilies of the Field and the Birds of the Air* and *Three Discourses at Communion on Fridays*. There then followed two works by a new pseudonym, Anti-Climacus: *The Sickness unto Death* and *Practice in Christianity*.

These two form the coping-stones of the life-view presupposed by and aimed at in the earlier pseudonymous writings. They are natural partners of the religious discourses among which they appeared (and more of which were to follow). They exploit the ambitious spiritual level of the discourses in order to throw light on the developing religious point of view of the earlier pseudonyms. In all Kierkegaard's later writings one detects a new stringency. The *Corsair* affair enforced a polarization between him and his society. His own suffering for truth was set off against the complacency of a bourgeois public and its religious leaders. Thus, in a way, the social and political criticism that emerged in the *Review*, which might have been Kierkegaard's final work, was a seed that developed in the atmosphere created by the feud with *The Corsair* to become a general condemnation of the age in which he lived, culminating in a vitriolic attack on the State Church, which he saw as the root and bastion of spiritual complacency. The remainder of his inheritance went into financing the final assault through his own broadsheet, *The Instant*. This went through nine issues before Kierkegaard fell ill, collapsed in the street, and died in hospital six weeks later, on 13 November 1855. He was forty-two years old.

NOTES

1. *Søren Kierkegaards Papirer*, vols. I–XI:3, ed. P. A. Heiberg, V. Kuhr and E. Torsting, 1909–48; suppl. vols. XII–XIII, ed. N. Thulstrup, 1969–70 (Gyldendal, Copenhagen), vol. VII:1 A 97 and 98, 9 March 1846 (*Papers and Journals: A Selection*, trans. Alastair Hannay (Penguin Books, Harmondsworth, 1998), pp. 213–17).

2. Søren Kierkegaard, *Papirer*, vol. VII:1 A 4, 7 February 1846, Hannay (trans.), *Papers and Journals*, p. 204.

3. Søren Kierkegaard, *Papirer*, vol. VII:1 A 9, 9 February 1846, Hannay (trans.), *Papers and Journals*, p. 204.

4. Søren Kierkegaard, *Papirer*, vol. VII:1 A 3, from 1846, Hannay (trans.), *Papers and Journals*, p. 203.

5. *To Tidsaldre* (*Two Ages*) (J. L. Heiberg, Copenhagen, 1845), p. v.

6. 'Glittering vices.'

7. Søren Kierkegaard, *Papirer*, vol. VII:1 B 135, from 1846, Hannay (trans.), *Papers and Journals*, p. 251.

8. Søren Kierkegaard, *Papirer*, vol. VII:1 B 43, from 1846, *Papers and Journals*.

FURTHER READING

For some useful literature in connection with *A Literary Review*, see the collection of essays devoted to *A Literary Review* in N. J. Cappelørn and H. Deuser (eds), *Kierkegaard Studies: Yearbook 1999* (Walter de Gruyter, Berlin and New York, 1999); H. L. Dreyfus and J. Rubin, 'Kierkegaard on the Nihilism of the Present Age: The Case of Commitment as Addiction', *Synthese* 98/1 (January 1994), pp. 3–19; H. Fenger, *The Heibergs*, trans. F. J. Marker, Twayne World Authors Series (Twayne Publishers, New York, 1971); A. Hannay, 'Kierkegaard's Present Age and Ours', in M. Wrathall and J. Malpas (eds), *Heidegger, Authenticity and Modernity: Essays in Honor of Hubert L. Dreyfus*, vol. 1 (MIT Press, Cambridge, Mass., 2000), pp. 105–22, notes pp. 354–6; G. Kjær, 'Thomasine Gyllembourg, Author of *A Story for Everyday Life*', in R. L. Perkins (ed.), *International Kierkegaard Commentary: Early Polemical Writings* (Mercer University Press, Macon, Ga., 1999), pp. 87–108; and G. Pattison, '*Poor Paris!': Kierkegaard's Critique of the Spectacular City*, Kierkegaard Studies: Monograph Series 2, ed. N. J. Cappelørn and C. Tolstrup (Walter de Gruyter, Berlin and New York, 1999).

For a comprehensive view of the wider background to Kierkegaard's writings in the context of his contemporaries, see B. H. Kirmmse, *Kierkegaard in Golden Age Denmark* (Indiana University Press, Bloomington and Indianapolis, 1990).

For general surveys of Kierkegaard's works and essays relating them to more recent thought, see A. Hannay and G. D. Marino (eds), *The Cambridge Companion to Kierkegaard* (Cambridge University Press, Cambridge, 1998); M. J. Matustik and M. Westphal (eds), *Kierkegaard in Post-Modernity* (Indiana University Press, Bloomington and Indianapolis, 1995); and J. Rée and J. Chamberlain (eds), *Kierkegaard: A Critical Reader* (Blackwell, Oxford, 1998).

For biographies see A. Hannay, *Kierkegaard: A Biography* (Cambridge University Press, Cambridge, 2001); W. Lowrie, *Kierkegaard* (Oxford University Press, London, New York and Toronto, 1938); and J. Thomson, *Kierkegaard* (Alfred A. Knopf, New York, 1973). For valuable biographical background material, see B. H. Kirmmse (ed.), *Encounters with Kierkegaard: A Life as Seen by His Contemporaries*, trans. B. H. Kirmmse and V. R. Laursen (Princeton University Press, Princeton, NJ, 1996).

TRANSLATOR'S NOTE

The following translation is based on the third edition of Kierkegaard's *Samlede Værker*, ed. A. B. Drachmann, J. L. Heiberg and H. O. Lange (Gyldendal, Copenhagen, 1963), which first appeared in 1901–06 and was revised in 1962. A new edition, *Søren Kierkegaards Samlede Værker*, ed. N. J. Cappelørn, J. Garff, J. Kondrup, A. McKinnon and F. H. Mortensen (The Søren Kierkegaard Research Centre and Gads Forlag, Copenhagen), is in progress. Several drafts of parts of the *Review* are to be found in Kierkegaard's *Papirer* (a selection of which is published in Penguin Classics as *Papers and Journals: A Selection*, trans. A. Hannay (Penguin Books, Harmondsworth, 1998)), some dating from before the completion of the manuscript of *Concluding Unscientific Postscript* and probably written just after the publication of *Two Ages* in October 1845. For reasons of a mainly stylistic nature, some of this material was not incorporated in the final version. Part of *A Literary Review* was translated by Alexander Dru as *The Present Age* (Oxford University Press, London, New York and Toronto, 1940), and a complete translation by Howard V. Hong and Edna H. Hong, with copious annotation, has been published as *Two Ages* (Princeton University Press, Princeton, 1978). The present English translation is the first to appear under a rendition of the original title.

I am most grateful to Jon Stewart for important matters of detail, to Laura Barber for good advice on drafting this introduction, and to Sue Phillpott for many linguistic, stylistic and other improvements throughout.

A Literary Review

Two Ages, a novel by the author of
A Story of Everyday Life, published by
J. L. Heiberg, Copenhagen, Reitzel, 1845

REVIEWED BY

S. KIERKEGAARD

This little publication
is dedicated
to the
UNNAMED YET SO FAMED[1] author of
A Story of Everyday Life

Preface

This review was originally meant for *Nordisk Literaturtidende*.[1] But its excessive length in relation to the modest compass of that paper, up to half of whose space is devoted to Swedish and Norwegian literature, soon became obvious to me, as also my incompetence when it comes to writing for periodicals. We have no journal of aesthetics: so, very well, let this circumstance be what the review itself will refer to occasionally as the unity of the surroundings' reflection and psychological consistency, in this case the unity of my being the author and the review therefore being disproportionately long, and of the fact that nowadays any reasonably adequate review has to be published as a book in its own right. It will quickly be seen in any case that this review is not meant for aesthetic and critical readers of newspapers but for rational creatures with the time and patience to read a little book, without this implying that this is one they should read. That the book is written for *them* puts them in no way under an obligation to read it; all it means, at most, is that those whose critical and aesthetic education comes from reading newspapers are excused from doing so.

S.K.

Introduction

Complaints of infidelity and faithlessness are frequent enough between one man and another, and the comedy all too imminent that, rather than marking a difference between them, what we have is an all the more faithful image of the respects in which they are alike, accuser and accused transformed in a new misunderstanding, the one still seeing himself as the accuser of the other, instead of each separately accusing himself and finding an understanding. However much, and however justly, one person reproaches another for infidelity, fickleness, inconstancy, he is careful not to put his own inconstancy down to the same reasons, for that would be to betray himself as someone having the law of his existence outside himself – and yet what else is variability? If it is true that time changes everything – whatever can be changed – it is also true that time will show who it was that did not change. So for every faithful and committed person, instead of complaints and accusations, settlements and court decisions, there remains the compensation that a second look will in time show whether or not he was unfaithful and whether the charge of infidelity had the power to change him or not. Ironically enough, the person quick to accuse another could sometimes almost wish, at the moment of reckoning, that the vehemence of his accusation had obtained the opposite effect to the one he had wanted at the time; because it is the accuser who proves now to have changed, and who perhaps now in a renewed vehemence resembles himself in complaining about this invariability. As seldom as pain, suffering and mortal danger are to be found where the screaming is, so too is faithfulness to oneself seldom found where another is being stridently accused.

The same is not infrequently true in literary affairs: an author accuses the age of infidelity and the age accuses the author of the same, either for what it takes to be a decline in his ability or, perhaps, for his seizing all too anxiously and frantically, in his attempt to meet the demands of the age, upon something that still does not satisfy it. Both sides can be at fault. But here again the second look will decide whether it is the author in question who has remained essentially true to himself, and the world that has changed, or whether he is an inconstant mind, 'a wandering star'[1] that wants to capture the changeable with change-ableness while nemesis captures him in his own snare.

In this, the situation resembles the one indicated above between man and man, except that special complications in literature make it dialectical; the two individuals stay in some factual sense the same, while an age, a reading public, has a quite other and dialectical character. An author just a little advanced in years, whether forgotten or familiar, quickly sees himself surrounded by a new influential age, whether not unreasonably entitled to the demands it makes or misled like that new pharaoh who knew not Joseph and his merits.[2] The changed age sometimes expresses its change by then accusing the author of being unfaithful to *his* age − which is suspect, particularly when it remains unclear what is to be understood by *his* age or *the* age; for then it is *eo ipso*[3] impossible for any author to end up other than by being unfaithful to his age just by remaining faithful to it, since *the* age is, sophistically, always the new replacement. The author, the individual person, who grows older with each year, can only be renewed within himself; he cannot become a new man with each age. If the seeming metaphysical profundity about the demands of the age isn't to dissolve in confusion, here again the second look must be assumed capable of judging ethically, by deciding whether we have an author who stayed true to himself despite the demands of the age; or one who betrayed himself and the commitments he publicly undertook and thereby stood in the way of the fulfilment of a justifiable demand; or, finally, whether we have a sleight-of-hand artist who ended up hoodwinking himself. For unless the ethical is granted a decisive say over all this reckless talk of the demands of the age, not just our own age but every age is guilty of unfair, ungracious and nonsensical behaviour towards all older authors.

Even if a power-hungry older generation will secure itself with a Bethlehem-style infanticide, a literary patricide is equally loathsome.*

Young people today can fairly often be heard saying wise things. That youth speaks you will hear sure enough on closer listening. For what a wise man doesn't fail to see – that everything he says is about himself (that's how selfish he is!) – the young man indeed fails to see (that's how enthusiastic he is!). What the wise man does, namely understand everything as being relevant to himself, always taking himself to be a case in point, the young man fails to do; he makes the demand but fails to implicate himself – or indeed, the demands he makes being what they are, he implicates hardly anyone else either. You would think it was a drunken deity speaking, from his free manner with people, from the way his head swims in a fantasy of supposedly being able to grab for himself the monster product of generations of inhumanly exacted exertion; least of all would you believe it was an individual human being speaking. Clearly, *he* certainly speaks in the name of *the age* concerning *the age*'s demands, but this is precisely the contradiction that ought to put a stop to the youngster's fairy-tale savagery; for no one, no fictional pirate captain, was ever so cruel as the demands of the age in the mouth of a young man; not even Elagabalus[4] was that terrible to the ostriches, for he never had more killed than he could eat.

Scantier and scantier are the rations allotted to those who excel; ever more quickly are suspicions aroused about being unfaithful to the demands of the age; in the young man's mouth ever new powers are demanded by the age. And this person who we suppose not to be making this demand *on* demand, who by being unfaithful to himself and to what it is to be human has in one way or another taken the

---

* This is something I may be in the very best position to claim, being myself a younger author who never, thank God, had anything to do with the demands of the age in the way of active service on its behalf. My experience with the demands of the age has been as with my military service: I got my discharge immediately and both times it was what I wanted. But by beginning with the discharge one always has the advantage of not becoming too deeply involved. [In his first student year Kierkegaard enlisted, as was the rule, in the King's Guard but was discharged four days later as physically unfit to serve. Trans.]

demand that demands faithfulness to be his *own* demand, this monstrous creditor who can offer no explanation whatsoever of how he came into possession of the demand but merely advances it – this person does not dream that the judgement he pronounces will be the one by which he himself is judged, yes, by an even severer judgement and a narrower standard.[5]

We see less often a sincere wish to learn from life but, correspondingly more often, people's desire and inclination and mutual encouragement to be deceived by it. Unabashed, people seem to lack any Socratic fear of being deceived. For the voice of God is always a whisper, and in the shape of a thousand-tongued rumour the demand of the age is not an almighty command that creates great men, but a stirring in the refuse that creates muddled minds; an abracadabra, as with all bringing forth, that brings forth its like. Even less do people seem, Socratically, to fear more than all else being deceived by themselves, and least of all do they realize that if of all the deceived the self-deceived are the most pitiful, then the most pitiful among these in turn are those who, in contrast to the piously deceived, deceive themselves presumptuously. Slow to listen, quick to judge,[6] they comply with only half of the Socratic teaching that one draw modest conclusions from the little one grasps,[7] for from the little they grasp they draw brazen conclusions. The momentary, a brilliant beginning, and a new time-reckoning dating from it are the little one grasps – if indeed it is possible to understand the momentary and the beginning inasmuch as the momentary lacks the eternal and, until the meaning is complete, the beginning lacks the conclusion; and one ought to wait for this for the sake not so much of the meaning as of the grasping. As for what comes next, there is no need of that, now that one speaks in the name of time, for time grasped in this abstract way is an extremely indifferent power; all will surely go well with it even should no young man concern himself on its behalf.

But those individual human beings, each of whom should have *his* time, what of them? For individuals something does come after, the consequent following that brilliant antecedent[8] – those happy days of youth when one was oneself the demand of the age. As for this next phase, the less time allotted the older ones, the more speedily it arrives upon us and the longer becomes the consequent – and the shorter the tiny antecedent, if indeed it doesn't dwindle to nothing at all because of the impossibility of grasping it together with the consequent. Truly a brilliant beginning for a new era! One cannot call it beginning with nothing,[9] more like ending with the beginning *becoming* nothing. Not even Pandora's box could contain so many disasters and so much misery as are concealed in that little phrase 'the demand of the age'.[10] Any person who has flirted with this phrase has only himself to blame; he can hardly complain about what the age demands when the demand is one he himself has made!

And yet people won't understand the sequel. In our concern to let ourselves be guided, to rejoice fervently and with admiration in the older person when he stays true to himself, to be edified by fifty years of faithful service, to grasp slowly, to learn from the venerated, from whom one learns something other than from the luminaries of the moment – we seem to lack the patience to learn in this way what it is to be human, and to renounce the inhuman. But might not this, too, be the demand of the age? Yes, and if it is not the demand of the age, it is still that of the power higher than the age, for it is the demand of eternity. If it is not the demand of men, it is the demand of God. If it is not the demand of the young, it is the demand of the Ancient of Days![11] And is it really fidelity to demand fidelity only in an inhuman way? Is it fidelity to make far greater promises than any human being can keep? And isn't comedy just around the corner in a conflict between two people one of whom made only an inhuman demand of fidelity without committing himself, so as to learn what human fidelity is, and the other of whom did commit himself but in such a way that fidelity proved impossible and infidelity that in which the antagonists resemble each other in the change?

But if this is how things are in general – and it is not very inviting – how refreshing then to focus attention on a phenomenon in which what is wanted comes together in mutual agreement; to allow one's own, perhaps a reader's, mind to dwell on what is dependable, to remind oneself, perhaps a reader, of what surely we all more or less clearly know. For if I mention *A Story of Everyday Life*, the occasion here is, fortunately for me, not the odious one of the hectic self-importance of a review, of directing attention, imposing the point of view; or by demonstrating the necessity of the development, of showing how the author here had to be a dramatist, there a natural scientist, etc. For me the occasion is the fond one of a happy repetition of a beautiful memory. The author has remained the same 'one in all'.[12] The reading public doesn't need to be informed, doesn't even need to be reminded, yet may still find pleasure in being put in mind of what it knew. Heaven knows there is constantly so much new to know that to be reading this will be almost a relief! No one, not even the most hotheaded youth, will expect in my mentioning *A Story of Everyday Life* to be witness to the court martial of a superannuated signature in the name of the age. But everyone in all fairness expects a review to be a solemn performance, as I too wish and hope; and if it proves not to be so I accept the blame in advance. If, as I am, one is firmly convinced that it is a reviewer's duty always to be a ministering spirit, even if on rare occasions he is far superior to the one he reviews, here it would be difficult for anyone to fall into temptation, and for me impossible. Not really being a contemporary of this author's debut, the truth is rather that I have grown up under him and, now his contemporary, I have not outgrown the impression he made then.

For close on twenty years there has been a happy relationship – one in which, as one says of marriages, the partners get along fine – between this author and the reading public. It is pleasurable to think of it and salutary for me to speak of it personally, even though what I say may be something different and again, in the difference, may mark the contrast between this author's life-view and a more pronounced religious view. A passionate religious enthusiast would focus exclusively on the author's faithfulness to himself and would, in his admiration, hear nothing of any relation to a reading public, nothing about the world, either its approval or its disapproval. He would exclaim: 'Splendid, here is something for us to learn; yes, everyone, author or not, can learn something from this, for everyone can learn from a universal paradigm, and being faithful to oneself is what is universally paradigmatic!' He would not say 'only twenty years' but 'for twenty years!'. But then the author of these stories – if I may be so bold as to make him the examiner while I submit myself to the examination, to show how and what I have learned from him – would caution the enthusiast not to skip over life's tribulations, not to make light of fortune's incentives to merit. He would no doubt remind him, echoing an expression employed earlier, that 'the road goes over the Bridge of Sighs'* then proceed to bid him let his 'moderation be known unto all men'[13] in resignation's quiet joy over life, which shows here precisely that things are just as we learn in the stories; yes, even better, that not only will everything surely come to rights again, little by little, but that everything was and remained good. And yet, however willingly that religious enthusiast submitted to this instruction and accepted the lesson, perhaps he might revert once again to his view, which after all did not overlook suffering, does not put a rash trust in the world, but religiously wants success and failure to mean equally much – that is, equally little – and wants the religious to have meaning not by way of and together with something else, but to have absolute meaning in itself.

The author has been true to himself. Were anyone foolishly to remark that he has been faithful over only a few things[14] because he hasn't busily changed the subject, because he hasn't explored all areas, because he has not juggled with a showy variety, I would answer this obviously trumped-up charge by saying, 'This is exactly where the author's great wealth lies.' The life-view creatively sustaining these stories remains the same, while an ingenious inventiveness, a reserve of material gained from a rich experience and a fertile luxuriance of mood, all serve to produce change within the creative repetition. The disquiet stays essentially the same, the reassurance essentially the same, essentially from the same to the same in all cases. The conflict introduced has essentially the same power to seek resolution, the peace and quiet are again the same – that is, it is the same life-view. If we take one of these stories in its entirety and then consider the others, and if as we are wont we call the writer's work a 'creation', I would rather describe the relation of the whole series to that one story with the single word 'sustaining'. But is God, with whom one compares a writer when he is called creative, less admirable in the sustaining than in the creating? So too with our author's continuing creation. Indeed, were it otherwise

---

* Cf. *From the Papers of One Still Living*, published by S. Kierkegaard, Copenhagen, 1838 [*Søren Kierkegaards Skrifter* (Gads Forlag, Copenhagen, 1997)].

with the author, his own works would contain a contradiction. The life-view in the one story must be contained again in the sequels, for any discrepancy will show that despite all his seeming creativeness the author has no life-view; this author, though, in heartfelt faithfulness, reproduces his own originality in the repetition. Were we to measure his talent with, as it were, a psychological meter, we would find it essentially the same in all the stories; if we were to 'log' the momentum of passion psychologically, we would find it essentially the same in them all. All have the same closeness to the reality of daily life and the same distance from it in elevation, the same closeness to the conflict and the same distance from it in understanding. This author is thus equally close to and distant from reality; closer to it in the apprehension than a poet, not as far from it as a poet in the idealized presentation, for the author's life-view lies on the outer boundary of the aesthetic veering towards the religious; where poetry to all intents and purposes stops, this author begins.

For the essence of poetry is not to achieve reconciliation with *the actual*, but to achieve reconciliation with the imaginative ideal through imagination. But in the actual individual this reconciliation is precisely the new split with reality. A knowledge of the pain of actual life, something poetry itself cannot bring out (because its dialectic of time and reality is less intense than that of despair), finds its reconciliation in a reassurance of a kind that poetry (*stricte sic dicta*)[15] cannot take hold of precisely because the reconciliation is with reality. All the same, in these stories the author never comes up with the kind of real-life pain that could find reassurance only in unmistakably religious categories and in the ideality[16] of religion. Every life-view knows the way out and can be recognized by the way out it knows. The poet knows imagination's way out, and this author knows reality's; the religious person knows religion's way out. The life-view *is* the way out and the story is the way. These categories themselves make it readily apparent that no one can bring about reconciliation with actual life in the way this author does, precisely because his way out *is* actual life. The mastery of the rendition lies in the fact that this is nowhere expressly stated but that it constantly happens, comes about, that the peace in which the story ends is achieved in the transparency of event and personality.

That this author was bound to achieve distinction by being true to himself is in any case not hard to explain psychologically, though the sublime ease of it all makes the fidelity no less admirable. *A Story of Everyday Life* (or *Stories of Everyday Life*) is easily recognizable as the fruit of a second maturity; which is exactly why there can be no question of the crises and crucial changes of direction inevitably experienced by an author entering upon his first maturity. The life-view sustaining *A Story of Everyday Life* (the first story, which gives its title to them all) must have matured in the author before he wrote it. His product isn't part of his own development, but the development being mature, the fruit it bears is a product in inwardness. It is not its genius, not talent, nor virtuosity that make the product what it is, for if that were so, the creative element in it would practically vanish were these to disappear. No, if anything, the very production, the possibility of being able to yield such a work, is the reward God has bestowed on the author, since, twice matured, he has gained something eternal in a life-view. It is because he is an author who isn't looking for himself, but one who found himself before he became an author, that he can be a guide. And whether or not one can repose in the same life-view oneself, here at least are the peace and incorruptibility of a quiet spirit.[17] Just as any message of heart-rending tragedy (and God knows how anyone thinks that might be put across!) is seldom to be found in the stories, neither is there any of that self-importance that arouses expectant curiosity about whatever is supposed to satisfy the demand of the age, which today's uneasy author complacently assumes to be whatever makes for happiness.

No, *A Story of Everyday Life* is not only a consummate story, it is the story of consummation itself. We begin reading it with pleasure, knowing already that here is the dependability of a life-view not about to be disturbed by a wandering star's vacillations, but under a guiding star's protection. Knowing the life-view in advance, we now rejoice to see it once more come into existence, changed but in repetition; a change not, with masks and mummery, inviting others inquisitively to snatch something new, but a change for inwardness. This has been going on for close on twenty years while the outward demeanour has remained the same: the same almost feminine resignation that nevertheless instils respect, the same modesty of approach, the same remoteness from the turmoil and demands of the age, the same domesticity and faithful adherence to a Danish reading public; and this, too, is so delightful – that *A Story of Everyday Life* is as good as untranslated into any foreign language: a contented and self-conscious joy over little Denmark! Oh, how delightful to be such an author, how delightful to be that celebrity who has appended his famous name as editor. Just like the stories themselves, those two also form an association in fidelity. The editor acquired no fame from them – he was famous already. But the stories, which have won a name of their own, next to the editor's one of the most important, continue to seek in the sacrifice of anonymity a place among the celebrated.

And the reading public has been true to the author. He has always been received with a welcome, and though he has never excited expectation, least of all unreasonable expectation, he has always been expected. That's how it was at the beginning when Professor Heiberg[18] assumed aesthetic command of Danish literature and tossed these stories episodically into *Flyveposten*'s exuberant, witty, edifying, instructive entertainment, in a way that deceived the eye and made it impossible to tell whether it was fact or fiction. By often reading *Flyveposten* and these stories in that evasive setting, younger people have tried to enter into the spirit of the enchantment that the stories must have exercised over contemporaries. The manner of their reception at the beginning was no different when, later, the stories came out so appealingly, year after year, at Christmas. For whatever objections there are to making such an adventitious season into a trade fair, and particularly for such an adventitious reason as a need for presents, as if Danish literature were nothing but a presentation literature,[19] it is never in that way that *A Story of Everyday Life* has arrived with Christmas. The special place it has acquired would have been enough to prevent any offensive misunderstanding, even if its plain and unassuming appearance didn't already, even at very first sight, preclude any misunderstanding. However sad it is that the Danish reading public is so small, this can still have its appealing side and enable an author, precisely by keeping his own person out of it, to enter in a congenial and friendly way into an almost personal relationship with his public.

That is how *A Story of Everyday Life* came at Christmas. It never struck anyone as a book that one bought; the price was more like a tip given to the bearer of welcome news, and the book really was a gift one accepted. People imagined, individually flattering themselves, that it was the author's own concern that made the book appear just at Christmas. In *Flyveposten* the reading public had seized upon *A Story of Everyday Life* in surprise, taken in by the ambivalent lighting and bamboozled by getting it only a little at a time. At Christmas it came as a welcome gift; looking forward to it was itself a pleasure, to receive what was expected no less so. It was received in the same way at every other time of the year, as now with the most recent issue that came out in November. Thus has it enjoyed its splendid continuity from the start. And where is the genuine reader of Danish literature who doesn't somehow have one or two of these short stories woven into his own life memories, whether as what the story means for himself or as what it means in a cherished situation? Young people have read it aloud, perhaps to this or that person; lovers have decided in advance to make the book a New Year gift; a housewife has in addition to a new silk dress every year insisted on the expected *Story of Everyday Life* annual; a lovers' quarrel has been patched up and marital tension eased by reading such a novel. It is also due to their very dependability, the foreknowledge that no actual relationship, neither love nor marriage, nor family, nor station in life, would be cast in a misleading light, but would on the contrary be clarified and made endearing, that these stories have contributed so much to interpersonal commerce and exchange.

But what power is it that this author possesses that enables him to do all this, if it is due neither to anything special in a particular novella nor to his superiority as a novelist? What else than the fact of his being a representative of a specific life-view? And it is precisely this extra that places him above novelists in general, an advantage quite different from whatever may be claimed for him by comparing him with others within the novelist category. Often, after making the acquaintance of seventeen characters in a story, hearing them talk, reading their correspondence, having been transported to so many places, picked up local knowledge and benefited from glorious vistas, one ends up none the wiser because the novel itself, taken as a whole, ends in a tangle because it lacks a life-view, and knowing all those characters provides no greater enrich-ment than getting to know seventeen people at a party. The acquaint-ance may be all very interesting but it does not illuminate life; one is confirmed in what one already knows about these people, or perhaps one finds a new individuality not quite as one finds in real life; but there is no illumination of the whole.

If a creative writer – and here it is not a matter of comparisons but of what marks someone out as being *essentially* a writer – is said to transport and inspire because it is essentially through imagination that he produces his effect, then I would say of the author of *A Story of Everyday Life* that he 'persuades'. The ability to captivate and entertain is less his distinguishing mark since the same can be said of the poet and of many other novelists. He *persuades*, and this too is a difficult but also beneficent art. If one likes to say that the poet (*stricte sic dictus*) has only high or low notes, and so cannot talk with people as they are in real life, then the life-view of the author of *A Story of Everyday Life* can be said to possess the middle note of persuasion, and the perfection of the enunciation of that life-view lies precisely in this. What we hear are not loud, animated, agitated calls to fight, to find pleasure, to flout life's opposition, nor cries of despair; nor do we see such scenes depicted, nor endings brought about by resolutions of the sort. Here the inviting intimacy of the cheerful inner sanctum opens its shrine to us, from which heated emotions, perilous decisions and excesses of exertion are excluded, since here such things can be neither accommodated nor tolerated.

Allowing oneself to be spoken to is a prerequisite of accepting the guidance of persuasion. This low-key compliance is the prerequisite, in turn, of persuasion's ability to elicit from low spirits a new harmony. Everything will be for the better again. By what means? Yes, ask it with due decorum, for even when you ask correctly, to ask vehemently renders impossible the assimilation of the answer. By what means? By the use of common sense, so as to gain for suffering a more merciful aspect; by having patience, a patience that expects good fortune to smile again; by the friendly sympathy of loving people; and by the resignation that renounces its claim not to everything, but to the highest, and through contentment transforms the next-best into something almost as good.

And none of this is put across – it just happens – and it is for this very reason that, if one gives oneself up to it, the persuasion is so powerful. No orator can persuade like this, simply because he has a motive, and contemplation always gives birth to doubt. Here, however, persuasion is not a matter between two persons but the pathway in the life-view, and the novel leads one into the world that that view creatively sustains. But, then again, this world is precisely the actual one; so you have not been deceived by the view; it has simply persuaded you to stay where you are.

For what is persuasion, how does one define this concept philosophically and affirm its noble meaning, remembering that here it is not a matter of a relation between two individual human beings but that of a life-view to its recipient? Persuasion presupposes a difficulty, an obstacle, an opposition. It starts with that, and then persuasion clears it away. Persuasion is a movement on the spot but one that changes the spot. Aesthetically, the individual is led away from the actual world and translated into the medium of the imagination; religiously, the individual is led away and translated into the eternity of the religious. In each case the individual becomes alien to the actual world. Aesthetically, the individual becomes alien to the actual world by being absent *from* it; religiously, the individual becomes an alien and a foreigner *in* the actual world. So a difficulty is presupposed, or the immediate internal coherence of happiness and immediacy is assumed to be broken. But the break does not end meaninglessly in despair, nor does it become the beginning of a qualitatively new life. As a broken flower is held up by its stalk until, though still bearing the mark of its fracture, it regains its strength, so too is this life-view the support that sustains the person who is broken until he raises himself up again. Yet precisely this is persuasion. Immediacy does not know what persuasion is because it has no need of healing, while religion is unable to persuade for the very reason that it presupposes a new beginning.

A Story of Everyday Life thus *persuades*, and here again is indicated the limit it does not want to transcend. If one wanted to combine with it a striving in the direction of the ultimate completion of the Idea, then the story would again be persuasion, but like a friendly, restraining force, while even the most unruly person will nevertheless not evade the responsibility of shunning that court of appeal.

No doubt many, captivated by its persuasiveness, have found their foothold in this life-view. And even if others demand more decisive categories, *A Story of Everyday Life* is still a resting place or, if you like, a place of prayer,[20] for a certain religious tinge is unmistakable simply because the life-view is not just common sense but common sense mitigated and refined by persuasive feeling and imagination.

But what am I saying? If someone *demands* more decisive categories? Am I not then speaking of the demand of the age? Instead of being one single human being, who like all such cannot be confused with the age, with criticism, etc., and so when faced with something like *A Story of Everyday Life* readily learns respect for it, have I not become an agitated party leader at the head of a revolt, stamping in the parterre and shouting the demand of the times? Happily not, and happily there is still something that *eo ipso* becomes nonsense when made into the demand of the times? For what can one not contrive to call the demand of the times? And is there anything that doesn't acquire a sort of prestige by being the demand of the times? But for decisive religious categories to become the demand of the times is *eo ipso* a contradiction.

Whereas, if one has any concern or inclination in this direction, one can in any case be hard put to it to decide whether this or that really is the demand of the age, the investigation here is briefer, and not one of fact as to whether it really is the case, for it is an impossibility that this should be the demand of *the age*. So even if it actually were the demand, it would still not be that so long as one also demanded that one grasp what it is one is demanding. As a claimant, 'the age' is too abstract a category to be able to demand the decisive religious categories, which belong precisely to individuality and particularity. You just cannot make en masse, collectively and noisily, demands for what can only fall to the single individual in particularity – solitariness, silence. Demanding has its own intrinsic dialectic too, so that the demands of the age should not be identical with the hue and cry of irrationality and be only appreciable in the human throng. Therefore no demand of the age can displace *A Story of Everyday Life*, as can be seen in the categories of individuality that underlie everything and in the use made of them in the stories. The single individual, or those who by becoming single individuals seek the decisive category of religiousness, will hardly be tempted to displace the persuasion; on the contrary, they will know to both honour and appreciate it. With regard to any tremor in the individuality that is ultimately only psychological, the life-view of *A Story of Everyday Life* is *eo ipso* one of consolation and recovery. And this is presented in these stories by such a master, endowed with such warmth and artistic skill, as to have reached its perfection. An individuality's spiritual tremor is *eo ipso* the indication of decisive religious categories, and spirit must therefore not be thought by any means identical with talent and genius, but with resoluteness in passion. A simple person can feel the need for the decisively religious, and even if a person of superior talent felt that need it would be very foolish to declare on that basis that he was an artist of the kind that is the author of these stories. Once religiousness in this way makes play with the word 'spirit', it has *eo ipso* ceased to be religiousness and become presumption.

A Story of Everyday Life has endured in this way for close on twenty years. To the older generation it has been an illumination of life or a corroboration of their understanding, and for the younger generation who have grown up with it, a guide – so what more natural a title for this new novel than *Two Ages*? But similarly, what more natural than an objection I would rather dispose of here, lest any suspicion arise that it might occur to me after I had read and reviewed the book to respond to anything of the kind? Objections are made to a book which in effect never gets beyond the binding and the title page, and which are therefore best answered, or more correctly disposed of, out of court. The problem here indeed appears on the title page, the difficulty is promptly rendered as an indictment of the book, and just as the Jews drained money from the country by way of bonds, so with similarly distorting conversions superficiality takes the pith and meaning out of literature. The puzzle is a difficult one. Yes; *ergo* it is not solved. No; whether it is solved or not is seen only by way of the book itself and a much more thorough inspection. The difficulty is this, that an older generation is undertaking to comprehend a more recent age. This is impossible, says the objection in passing, and concernedly shakes its head. Objections of this sort become all too easily popular, since every garrulous barber, even if he did not father it, gladly serves as its godfather.

It's an impossibility, goes the objection, because an older generation is always on the side of its own age and cannot understand ours. But this can also be turned around: a younger generation wants to understand an older – *ergo* its understanding fails because a younger generation is *eo ipso* on the side of its own age.

What does this mean? Translated into sensible language it means: this is a difficult problem. The reason I let this objection appear here was, in case some nimble wit hurriedly got to work promoting it *cito citissime*,[21] to usher it to its seat, transformed, certainly, as is the transformed title itself – transformed into a fitting and respectful admission of the difficulty of the problem. An objection like this can, in this way, even though in alien service, still be of some use; and it also suitably concludes the Introduction, in case anyone finds what I am about to add to it inappropriate. The first thing I ever wrote contained among other things some words in review of, or more correctly, in an effusive discourse upon, those novellas.[22] I have not tried my hand as a reviewer since. It is my wish, after seven years, to make a second and last attempt, again using a story of everyday life. I would hazard the guess, as far as decorum permits in connection with an anonymous author, that the honoured unknown author did read my little piece at the time. Should he honour me again by reading these lines, I hope he will find me unchanged or, if possible, changed in the repetition: a little more clarity in presentation, a slightly lighter and more flowing style, in recognition of the difficulty of the task a little less hurried, a little more inwardness in the discernment: in other words, changed in the repetition.

1 Prospectus of the Contents of Both Parts

Part One: The Age of Revolution

In the Copenhagen merchant Waller's home the arrival in the city of the French legation, and the reception into his family of these envoys along with other Frenchmen, was epoch-making. Waller[1] is a republican; his brother, *Counsellor of Justice W.*, 'whom the hard times have made prematurely hard to please',[2] is a royalist; his son *Ferdinand W.* is a republican; and for Supreme Court lawyer *Dalund*, a daily guest in the house, it is impossible to keep his neutral position as observer of these world-historical events, because each of the heatedly contending parties grasps his separate utterances with fervour and wrongly represents him as an advocate of his own party line. But while attention is directed in this way towards the great events and the Waller house is frequent witness to political disputes, concealed beneath all this is a secret understanding between *Madame W.*[3] and the lawyer Dalund. What the arbour and pastoral tranquillity do for the birth of innocent, or at least of forgivably errant, love, the distraction of great events does for the persistence of the forbidden love.

Finally, also visiting the Waller home is a young girl, *Claudine*, daughter of the merchant's sister. And among the Frenchmen there is one, *Charles Lusard*, in whom the young girl, brought up in virtual oppression by her aunt Malfred, soon finds an object for her now unfettered adoration. A banquet at the merchant's provides the high point of the political celebrations in the Waller home, and the beginning of an intimate understanding between Claudine and Lusard.

Although Part One of the novel is entitled 'The Age of Revolution', attention is now decisively focused on Claudine, so that the main motif seems forgotten unless it is remembered that C. precisely falls victim to the Idea of her age (p. 79), but is also restored in that Claudine is the one who better than any remained true to that Idea (p. 159). Thus the intriguing and yet so modestly chosen subject comes to light, 'the revolutionary age's life reflected in domestic life' – yes, the age of revolution reflected in a poor, abandoned woman's hidden seclusion deep in the country.

Lusard gets into a duel; wounded, he is brought in a fishing boat to the Waller country house where, in the most agonizing suspense, Claudine has suffered and continues to suffer all the terrors of a secret love affair, but is also maturing in the special inwardness of enamourment. L. stays on at the Waller country house, where he recovers; but, also, there in the rural quiet the understanding between him and Claudine reaches its climax, favoured by the situation and guided, as it were, by Ferdinand W.'s report of an illicit relationship between Madame W. and Dalund, as well as by his amplifications on the age's frivolous views about marriage.

Lusard goes off to the army leaving Claudine behind in the situation prophetically foretold by Ferdinand: 'that the memory of this should be enough to fill the life of a woman who knew how to love and appreciate what is glorious' (p. 20), a prophecy which in general may be untrue of any or, if true, only of the uncommon girl.

Already isolated in her sole possession of the knowledge of her relation to Lusard, Claudine becomes increasingly alone. Ferdinand W. writes a small collection of poems (*Primula veris*) containing revolutionary ideas, to his father's distress and concern, whereupon Ferdinand goes abroad. Waller goes to Amsterdam on business, accompanied by his wife. The venture succeeds but a mishap delays the merchant's return. Claudine's position becomes more and more desperate. She has no one in whom to confide in her misery, and finally decides to write to Madame Waller and reveal everything to her. The letter is sent off but arrives too late, for news is now received that Madame W. is dead. Dalund decides in his grief to go abroad; he informs Claudine of this in a note and hints despairingly at suicide. Driven to extremity, Claudine resolves in despair to end her own life. She is saved by the old housekeeper Susanne, and with the latter's help finds sanctuary with the old widow of a sea-captain. With no other resort in the world, Claudine now belongs wholly to her infant baby, with such a quiet dedication and sacredly *genuine* motherliness that 'the mother in her faithfulness had to succeed in atoning for the irresponsible mistake of the maiden' (p. 99), the warmth of her devotion having a kind of retroactive power to re-illuminate her lapse in a conjugal light.

Sure enough, Waller has received Claudine's letter to his deceased

wife, opened it and learned everything. He demands that Claudine
leave his house. An offer of marriage from Germany is negotiated by
the aunt and refused. Under the pretence of travelling to Germany,
Claudine leaves the city, alone with the infant, and moves to the
country, to her new hiding place where under the name of Madame
Johansen she lives unrecognized, forgetting the world and forgotten.
She hears nothing from Lusard – due as much to the cover-up itself as
to accidental circumstances, although some information about Lusard
does reach Waller.

Held in thrall in her faithfulness to herself and her child to the
memory of Lusard, whether dead or unfaithful, Claudine lives for
nine years in idyllically protected remembrance, only troubled and
touchingly embarrassed whenever she is led to explain how she happened to become a widow so young, whether to a simple farm woman
who asks in all innocence, or to a baron out of erotic interest, or to
little Charles in his childish naïveté. A baron whose former dissoluteness
bends to the power of love proposes to her and opens up for her the
prospect of a splendid future, which can also provide a cover for her
lapse. He unnerves her with his passion but gets a refusal; although
*dis*honoured, Claudine chooses to remain 'true to her husband and her
honour'.

Claudine is recognized by an outside party who is visiting the baron,
and recognized again by someone she is happy to see: Ferdinand W.,
who in the meantime has married and become a partner in a big
company in Switzerland, and on returning has learned from Susanne of
her whereabouts. He brings news that Lusard is living in Jutland as the
Duc de Montalbert, on an estate inherited from his uncle, a zealous
royalist, with whom at the time, in Claudine's interests, he had vainly
sought to be reconciled. Ferdinand W. brings news in turn to Lusard,
who believes C. unfaithful and to be married and living in Germany.
F. conveys his news as delicately as possible, so that the reunion be not
a poor, reluctant admission but an enthusiastic repetition; not as the
French song puts it about spring, a time . . . 'qui ne revient plus pour
les amants, comme il revient pour la nature'.[4]

Lusard and Claudine are reunited.

Part Two: The Present Age

Just as Claudine's trusty perseverance has been fidelity's triumphant path to the final reunion with Lusard, so this fidelity repeats itself in a rememorative perseverance that in its noble-minded wistfulness harks *back* to the union to which Claudine looked *forward*. The son, *Charles Lusard de Montalbert*, now fifty years old, lives in the magnificent old castle ('where for ten summers now the two big chestnut trees by the church wall have strewn their blossom')[5] – itself a reminding of the departed. After much travelling in the New World as well as the Old, having let the time of love pass by, having turned off at the point where a person's future really begins, [he] has beautifully installed himself in remembrance and chosen the past, wanting only to secure a memory for himself in making one member of his family happy.

Lusard comes to Copenhagen, visits *Commercial Counsellor Waller*, who lives in the old Waller house. Through the counsellor we are introduced to his marital confusions and to the stage upon which the present age reveals itself in its various representatives. The present age has nothing foreign with which to captivate, no legation of Frenchmen letting one virtually forget that the setting is Copenhagen and not the mighty upsurge of a world-historical denouement. Life in the present age is undisturbed by the energetic passion whose form is in its very energy – yes, even in its vehemence – and isn't hiding the power of a secret and forbidden passion. On the contrary, everything is manifestly nondescript, and thus trivial, formless, knowing, coquettish, and openly so. Here there is no great revelation and no deep secret, but superficiality all the more.

Just one flower, constrained by all these externalities, grows in concealment: Miss *Mariane*, a daughter of Counsellor Waller's first marriage, called in stepmotherly fashion 'Maren'[6] in the second marriage, even by the servants. Offended and ignored by the stepmother, vain object of her father's powerless protection, as good as insulted by young dandies whom the stepmother coquettishly flatters, and worried by her younger sister *Colette*'s schoolgirl irresponsibility, she secretly loves and is loved by *Ferdinand Bergland*, a grandson of Ferdinand Waller (author of *Primula veris*), a bit of an eccentric yet proud and refined.

Lusard soon discovers this girl's endearing character and is confirmed in his judgement by the old *Counsellor of State Dalund*, who now visits the house of Waller, an elderly man of whom one cannot say he had not chosen remembrance – that of Madame Waller – but that he preserved it; an elderly man who, just as he once vainly tried to maintain his neutral position as observer, now with his mild yet somewhat sarcastic outlook vainly takes up the cause as 'advocate for a vanished age – or against a present one'.[7]

No one knows where Ferdinand Bergland is. After a falling-out and misunderstanding with Counsellor Waller, he is thought to have left for Geneva. Mariane now becomes the designated object of Lusard's attention (misconstrued by some as if he himself were the wooer); her lover is earmarked as Lusard's heir. Despondently Lusard discovers, as he thinks, that Mariane is in love with *Arnold*, a law student whose emptiness repels Lusard. But Dalund denies that it is possible.

Lusard accidentally overhears a conversation between Mariane and her beloved – it is in fact Ferdinand Bergland, who has come home to say goodbye – whom he cannot see because he is hidden by the trees in the arbour, but whose voice and a signet ring catch his attention. Lusard learns from the conversation that the love affair is on the brink of breaking up; that the lover, fearing for his ability to provide, does not want to risk marriage but will give her up, hoping that Lusard will propose to her.

But who is this man? At a book auction Lusard buys the little volume, *Primula veris*, for twenty-five rix-dollars,[8] and his curiosity is aroused as to who could be the second bidder at that exorbitant price. From the voice and signet ring he now recognizes the lover from the arbour – it is none other than Ferdinand Bergland, the man they are looking for.

Just as a separation similar to that in Part One is about to occur; just as a loyal womanly soul (like Claudine) is about to be abandoned by her lover, not one who wishes to go to war (like [the first] Lusard) but one who helplessly dare not risk marriage for fear of his inability to provide; and just as the horoscope might indeed be set in such a way that Mariane would, like Claudine, remain faithful to herself over the years, but with less enthusiasm and animation and in silent, secret suffering – Lusard comes on stage. The remembrance of Part One once more casts its illuminating light. What filial piety wistfully remembers, the noble spirit now sees before him in a rejuvenated repetition.

Mariane is united with F. Bergland; they live in the old castle, the children and heirs of the solitary Lusard.

(1) In the arbour the candles are alight while in the twilight the star of love twinkles. Claudine is sitting with Lusard, and Ferdinand Waller is reading aloud a poem from *Primula veris*. (2) In the arbour the candles are alight – Ferdinand W. is sitting with little Madame Johansen and remembering what has never been forgotten. (3) In the arbour the candles are alight, and the shimmering stars look in through the leaves. Ferdinand Bergland is reading aloud to his wife, and Lusard is listening – he is reading from *Primula veris*.

Why is autumn the most beautiful time to fall in love? Why should 'September be called the love-month' (see Part One, p. 55)? Because it is in tune straight away with remembrance!

Ferdinand has finished reading; memories that linked him personally to that little book, and of the age whose ideas influenced it, have been reawakened. The two ages touch each other once again at the conclusion. Ferdinand B. says: 'I am happy to live in an age that despite its deficiencies makes such great advances in so many directions. I subscribe to the faith that the human race, no doubt through many fluctuations, will with steady stride nevertheless approach the goal of that perfection that can be imagined for an earthly existence.' And Lusard says: 'Amen, yes, we would hope for that.'[9]

The age of revolution's reflection in domestic life, the reflection of the present age in domestic life, is depicted but not judged, and hope is therefore not denied it either.

II An Aesthetic Reading of the Novel and Its Details

In summarizing the content I have tried to bring out the main elements in the development of the story, but also to interweave into the account the essential mood of the novel and by interposing certain adjectives to bring to mind what the conversations between the various characters are about. Finally, in line with the story, I have tried all along to let the totality of the age provide an undercoating, as it were. For what distinguishes this from other novels is its more substantial grounding: each part its age in its specific difference. A novel usually has only the pictorial background, like the line the illustrator dashes off over which to draw a figure; the drawing itself is what is produced, while the ground merely prevents what is drawn from looking as if suspended in the air. In this case, however, the novel is more universally grounded in something that is even more essential than what is presented, while what is presented is meant only to provide the reflection [*Gjenskinnet*]. The novel has as its presupposition the distinctive totality of the age, and what is brought out is that age's reflection [*Reflex*] in domestic life. After the presentation the mind turns back to the age's totality as now also revealed in this reflection. But the age itself is something the author (according to the Preface) has not wanted to present; his novel lies midway between the age's presupposed distinctiveness and that distinctiveness now illuminated in the reflection by the presentation.

The rule for the aesthetic critique, therefore, will not be whether or not you would find a girl like Claudine, a man like Lusard, like Dalund, etc., in our time. How unreasonable! The greatest departures can occur in any age; in ours there might be a man, for example, who could be said to belong really in the Middle Ages or in Greece. No, the critique's question is: can a girl like Claudine *typically* occur just in that age? Similarly with Part Two. The question is not whether a girl like Mariane could have lived in the age of revolution, thinking, feeling and acting as she does. The question is: can such a feminine figure *typically* occur in the present age?

Aesthetically, it is particularly in Part Two that the author develops his mastery in portrayal and description, his powers of observation, the dignified balance in his faithful reproduction of reality, in which he knows how to preserve even the worst foibles and vulgarities in such a way that they remain what they are, triviality and rudeness, and with such truth that it becomes interesting for that very reason. Even the most insignificant minor character in Part Two, where really there is no important character at all, comes alive to the reader, becomes so transparent in the few lines of conversation that the detail and the whole, through the very realism and vividness, produce a striking likeness. Only this author's sense of proportion, his interest in actual people in the context of the life-view, and his real concern, can explain what is so amazing: his ability to present all these characters in such a way as not for a moment to make one really laugh at them, even though most of them are such that they couldn't help but appear comical in the light of a purely aesthetic standard,* and would in the light of a purely ethical notion have to be condemned, if I may so put it, as counterfeit editions of human beings.

If one were to speak, in the kind of objection a hasty critique promptly puts into circulation, of the author's possible preference for one age over the other, closer inspection would on the contrary reveal *a specific expression of impartiality.* The author's possible preference for the revolutionary age's more animated life is balanced by the actual preference he has shown for the present age through his greater artistry

---

* Even a character like Mrs Waller, Commercial Counsellor Waller's consort, is only once made to appear comical in the book [p. 255, *trans.*], but to perfection, in that she embodies the kind of superficiality that consists in faithfully repeating anything at all, regardless of its aptness in context. Counsellor Dalund has accused our age of dalliance and said this is demonic. What happens? One day the lady surprises a young equerry (a friend of the family with whom she herself dallies) on the point of embracing and kissing a maid. The maid is dismissed and the equerry violently denounced, and it is here that the lines about dalliance and its being demonic are parodically inserted. What makes the comic construal even more superb is that the scene itself is not presented but reported by the little Colette, who repeats what old Dalund has said. The situation contains a wonderful irony at the extremely unfortunate choice of words, for in the event Dalund might well have been prepared to forgive the whole episode with the maid if it had gone unnoticed, while dallying is exactly what happens in the scene between Mrs Waller and the equerry, with whom she is coquettish. The satire implicit in a silly woman's repeating an old man's solemn words is excellent, as also is its casting light on Mrs Waller's capacity for improvement.

in depicting it. In Part One the plot is as simple as possible. After a few episodes in the Waller home, the story so to speak emigrates with Claudine and gets lost along with her in idyll, advancing slowly in an epic narrative manner until the reunion with Lusard. The episode with the baron, even in terms of compositional ingenuity, is so unsurprising that it falls a bit flat, being the kind of dramatic collision in which even a beginner usually tempts his heroines. The dramatic element in Part Two, on the other hand, is far more prominent. Here there is greater change and variety in the more complex situations; the tension in the development is maintained to the last and deceptively prolonged by Lusard's misapprehension of the relation between Arnold and Mariane, then cleverly brought to its resolution by an accidental event that lets Lusard in on the lovers' secret; and finally, beautifully resolved by inserting a situation that makes use of something the reader knows from Part One, while Lusard, seeing that it is what he has wanted from the beginning, does not appear as a *deus ex machina*. So what we find here isn't the usual financial help provided in novels, a rich uncle who gets killed off or most conveniently exchanges time for eternity, or same brought back with great speed from the East Indies, etc. On the contrary, the situation here can just as easily be reversed, and the problem is this: a noble man of means whose frame of mind is motivated by all of Part One, who seeks an object, and who in the story Guidance now helps to find the right two. Nothing is left unexplained, to foster doubt – no residual debt that can only be covered by a poetic advance from the huge relief fund of imagination. On the contrary, the mood at the point of resolution becomes a union of the outburst that marvels lyrically at the ways of Guidance and of the acquiescence of the understanding, which says: it could not be otherwise.

Another specific expression of impartiality is that the characters of Part Two stand out far more clearly, audible in the cues that their lines give, visible in the character sketches, and easily recognizable from life, while the characters in Part One are more hidden in the inwardness of a more universal passion. Although this has a deeper basis, the author's mastery consists precisely in his ability, in presenting them, to give difference its due – yet unobtrusively, never saying directly what he intends but knowing quite well what he has done. And what he has done the critique can straightforwardly state. The *difference* expresses in essence the relation between *inwardness* and the *weakness for showing off*, a malady of which the present age is often accused. It is a psychological principle on whose accuracy I am sure anyone of experience will agree with me, that in the presence of a genuine passion expressing itself in word and deed, the expression itself so captures attention as to make one forget the outer appearance; similarly, the person who genuinely experiences passion forgets the object of his passion's outer appearance. The ugliest person, if one is charmed by the warmth of his utterance, can make one entirely forget his external appearance. It was the irony of this contradiction that so gratified Socrates: when he spoke, when his listener Alcibiades' 'heart pounded violently, more violently than the Corybants', while tears streamed from his eyes',[1] it was forgotten, eternally forgotten, that the speaker was the ugliest man in Greece – until he fell silent, and the ugliest man in Greece savoured the irony of it all. If you have listened properly to a sermon brim-full of inwardness, even if your gaze has been fixed on the pastor, you will find it impossible to describe the pastor's appearance. Let a girl with heartache seek one's confidence; let her, in the eternal remembrance, possess grief's inwardness; on leaving her it is impossible to say how she looked, for the inwardness lets one forget in order to remember what is essential. Outwardness, on the other hand, forces itself upon one, making it impossible to forget because there is nothing to *remember*. A person really in love may for some time continue to be unable to explain just how his beloved looks; the superior power of his passionate inwardness makes him forget her appearance when he doesn't see her, for the simple reason that it is his being in love that he remembers. And at the same time he can easily form pictures of all who belong to the loved one's family and circle.

So it is with the characters in Part One of this novel. Practically all of them are in a state of passion, and for that reason stand out less sharply. Perhaps the most prominent in outward respects is Counsellor of Justice Waller, precisely because he is the least significant. The others are less clear to the degree in which they essentially possess the passion of an ideal, are absorbed in the universal life of a world-historical event, or concealed in the internal revelation of a self-generated passion. In

Part Two, on the other hand, practically all the characters have some recognizable outer trait that appeals to the imaginative memory. So clearly are they presented in the few strokes in which they are sketched that one cannot possibly forget them, and one would undertake confidently to recognize them on the street, because they are true-to-type stage extras of outwardness who altogether lack what makes one who remembers forget how they look. There is a pastor whose outward appearance I shall never forget, not just because he was undeniably handsome, but because he preachified so much that there was nothing to draw attention away from his appearance. Isn't this how it is? Imagine a fine lady who has taken special pains with her mourning preparations; one will be able to recall every fringe, every embellishment on her condolence-seeking countenance. But the young girl who really had the inwardness of sorrow – her appearance is something one could not recall.

Let us take Commercial Counsellor Waller.* He sits in the same office, at the same desk where his father sat before him, on a swivel chair, and 'looks like someone pestered by a swarm of flies on a hot summer day'.[2] Even if the author had presented him only once, we would never forget him, for his singularity is essentially outwardness. Let us take his lady Mrs Waller in her flirting, or when she comes on decked out in a bright shawl interwoven with gold. We don't forget how she looked. We compare this with the festivities in Waller's house, where Claudine appears wearing the tricolour sash,† and notwithstanding that this moment is frequently recalled, again we forget how she

---

* I cite, in the interests of brevity, just a few examples, but I cannot resist mentioning how the more one reads this novel the greater is one's admiration for the author's skill in making the situations offer superb opportunities for comparison, and for the unselfconscious art with which he conceals this so that the situation is so perfectly placed in the context of its Part that the last thing you would think was that it was intended.
† There is the additional difference that in Part One it is the merchant, Waller, who wants his wife and niece to adorn themselves with the nationally symbolic gifts the Frenchmen have had sent to him, for which liberty the [Frenchmen] graciously apologize to the women at that festive evening; while here it is the commercial counsellor's wife who has received a gift, and from a dandy who bought it because he was forced to and who gave it to the lady to get rid of it – and she wears it against her husband's wishes, while Mariane sees with pain that little Colette imitates her mother and accepts gifts from some man in the street.

looked; convinced of her beauty, we glance indifferently at the finery and forget, because our attention rests primarily on the romantic enthusiasm of the girl's youthful joy. Who remembers a gold case's appearance when it includes some curious inner feature in its construction! But a presentation salver, a name-plate, has, on the contrary, the characteristic that if one forgets the appearance one has completely forgotten the object. Similarly here. Both Madame W. with the little tricolour emblem carefully concealed, and the blissfully happy Claudine festively wearing the ribbons of the revolution, are genuinely decked out. This is not the case, on the other hand, with the wife of the commercial counsellor, with her gold belt or her sleigh-ride shawl interwoven with gold. And yet the irony of it is that one forgets how the first two looked just as one continues to remember them, but one never forgets the counsellor's wife with her belt – that is, if one does not forget her altogether.

Let us take Arnold and the scene (p. 262) where with his assumed ironical impertinence he insults the commercial counsellor in his own living-room; we compare it with the quarrel in Part One where Counsellor W. goes so far as to say: 'Those are slanderous words you are using.'[3] One forgets, beyond the significance of the topic, how the antagonists look; one forgives the impassioned man his violent outburst. But Arnold leaps out so clearly, one cannot be quit of him; there is nothing to help one forget, it all revolves around nothing and Arnold presents himself as the smug representative of emptiness and conceit whose irony is admired and prized by the commercial counsellor's wife. Take the scene in the arbour in Part One where Ferdinand W. talks away cheerfully about the relationship between Madame W. and Dalund in the presence of Claudine and Lusard; we find it unseemly but forget it almost immediately just because there is something to remember. Ferdinand is impassioned, he is carried away, misled by his modern ideas. Claudine is not inquisitive but, in the passion of infatuation, a light that is both disquieting and tempting dawns upon her. We compare it with the scene in Part Two where Arnold brings an invitation to Mrs Waller and where her relation to the equerry becomes the subject of coquettish discussion. Yes, it cannot be helped, the whole situation thrusts itself upon our memory. But who deserves credit? Yes, the author, who knows what needs to be done and how to do it. For the scene in Part One is one that even a beginner could have presented. There is no dialogue; it is Ferdinand W. who enthusiastically unburdens himself. But in Part Two we find this mastery in reproducing the commonplace, these brief rejoinders, the constant interweaving of situation into the lines; this exactness in even the most casual gesture, this animation, this play of colours, even though it is all quite properly kept in the vacuous shade of triviality. Let us take Colette, Arnold, the equerry, all representatives of the present age, who all so clearly and unforgettably represent themselves.

Where essential passion is present in inwardness, *the surroundings are forgotten*. In Part Two, however, with trained hand the author shows great care (simply from a predilection for the task) in sketching the daily circumstances of the workaday world. Here there is no hurrying to the important festive occasion, here one does not shut oneself up idyllically together with an abandoned woman's quiet inwardness. No, here everything is more or less equally important, making the rendition difficult, rather like painting without light and shade yet still producing an effect and a work of art. So we are not catapulted without further ado into the drawing-room, where flights of spirited talk and animated conversation and the good tone of cultured companionship bring pleasure – no, the author knows his job. From outside the drawing-room we hear the squabbling inside; we wait outside while the wife makes music; with one foot almost on the stairs the commercial counsellor's wife already begins to scold the equerry; the maid joins in the act, then small children and a schoolgirl – just because no sense of decorum distances or separates, nothing sublime elevates or marks out; no great event stimulates or ennobles, no idea marshals the masses in picturesque harmony, or raises the individual to heroic stature – everything is betwixt and between.

Briefly, the author's impartiality in relation to the two Parts might be put as follows: if Part One *captivates* more with the authenticity of great passions, then Part Two is more *entertaining*, especially the more one reads it.

So much for the impartiality. Another question is just how far this novel subscribes to the same conception of human existence as belongs essentially to *A Story of Everyday Life*. The latter's view lies, as was mentioned before, midway between the aesthetic and the religious. Let us, then, consider the relationships to existence of the main characters in the novel to hand. In Part One, the turn of the plot in the relationship between Claudine and Lusard is constructed *romantically* through *perseverance*; she bears up and gets Lusard. And her perseverance is in the main a natural endowment, a matter of immediacy and romantic love; for the ethical, in the form of the notion that Claudine can save her honour only by honouring herself, and that every new association, every irregularity that diminishes inwardness, is therefore a judgement upon herself, plays no decisive supporting role. Hers is a straightforward romanticism, not one transformed and sanctified by the ethical. The separation from Lusard puts her in a state of suspension, a state in which she remains at the romantic front and heading in Lusard's direction; she does not, by an ethical deepening within herself, raise herself above the relationship with Lusard while still holding the romantic desire's course towards the reunion with him. In Part Two, the turn of the plot in the relationship between Mariane and Ferdinand is developed *romantically* with the help of *fate*: Lusard comes along with financial assistance. The only question is whether it would have been closer to the spirit of the older story of everyday life to portray the baron (in Part One) a little differently and then have him united with Claudine; and have Mariane suffer the pain of separation, then to provide her with a new consolation.

But this comment, even if its correctness is conceded, in no way counts as an objection, since what the author is doing is rendering the two ages. Even less can one charge the author with trying, in the relation between Madame W. and Dalund in Part One, to give the natural side of the relationship the upper hand over the ethical, as though *staying true in an impermissible* relationship could make it permissible; nor can one object to the author's making the relationship look as if it even had an *ennobling* effect on Madame W. in her conjugal life with her husband, for this after all is a rendering of the special character of the age. Likewise when, in Part Two, breaking an engagement for fear of financial difficulties is made to seem a legitimate expression of passion. *Ethically*, the *former* must be regarded as *reprehensible* and the ennobling as an illusion; for no entitlement in any relationship can be acquired on the basis of what is forbidden – and the age of the offence is only its being repeated – because ennoblement through depravity is like the noblemindedness shown by a man who cannot get along without money, acquires his wealth unlawfully, and then does a lot of good with it. *Aesthetically*, the *latter* must be interpreted as *comical*. In Part Two, the present age too passes judgement on the relationship between Madame W. and Dalund, while the author is prevented by the nature of his task from disclosing his own views. Had there been yet another age it is not inconceivable that, in a rendition of it, that age would have seen Bergland's intended flight from marriage as comical.

I shall now, in an attempt to convey the author's splendid characterization, follow the development in the several main figures psychologically, showing how and to what extent crucial events turn on their basic individual outlooks, and allowing myself only a sideways glance at the age's reflection. The next section [III] must be reserved in the main for stressing the special characteristics of the age. The critique must adopt the same dual approach through which the story has made its own task so difficult. Nothing of the age itself can be allowed by the author to have an effect on the individuals directly, for then he would overstep the limits of his task as novelist; he would be describing the age itself and *illustrating it by examples* instead of apprehending the reflection of it in domestic life and illustrating it through that.

Human exchange must always occur by way of the middle term of the individual's psychology. For the author simply to say, 'In the revolutionary age a woman was allowed, if she otherwise observed decorum, to have an illicit relationship with a man – that's what I have presented in the relationship between Madame W. and Dalund', would be wrong. The relationship between Madame W. and Dalund must be psychologically motivated, and only then can there be talk of the special character of the age influencing it by imparting this particular expression to it, and of it being the special nature of the age that makes finding it permissible possible. It can happen in any age that a young girl falls in love with a man from whom she hears nothing for a long time, so that she believes him lost, and then marries, until the object of her first love reappears – doubly dangerous because she does not feel happy. If this is the case, and if, besides, the characters are portrayed psychologically, then the distinctive character of the age can be decisive in determining what expression this collision acquires. In another age it might have been expressed, for example, by the marriage finishing up on the rocks, so that she could get her beloved, or by the unhappy lovers' deciding in deference to the sanctity of marriage never to see each other again, etc. The author may not say, 'The age of revolution was an age of romantic girls and I have presented this in Claudine.' No, the author must motivate Claudine's romanticism psychologically, and after that it can be the age that determines the particular direction it takes. A romantic girl similarly motivated in the Middle Ages would have entered a convent; in a prosaic age she would have sighed, and married; in the period of Louis XIV she might have become a dubious countess, etc.

Claudine. Prudishly brought up by Aunt Malfred and thus intellectually both backward and precocious, well-nigh cheated of any impression of life and now transplanted to the merchant Waller's household, she has found the soil and season for her growth. What psychologically might have ended either in a stunting or in a despairing bursting of the bounds of the narrow-minded aunt's tight-laced parlour, is now happily transformed into the full bloom of youthful joy under the most favourable conditions possible, even if they might be called dangerous. The freedom she enjoys in the Waller house, the joy so abundantly offered, the sympathy and solicitude, almost partiality, shown for the young girl, do not spoil her – because she has learned discernment – but refine her in her childlike gratitude 'for all the blessings she enjoys in this dear household'.[4] And when the double doors are opened upon the broad prospect of a world-historical event, when the French legation, the emissaries from that enchanted stage, appear in the Waller house and brush Claudine's youthful mind magically with an idea, she is at her most sublime. The romantic is implicit in this brushing that coaxes the imagination. If Waller and his wife had travelled to Paris and taken Claudine with them, it wouldn't have had nearly so great an effect on her as that glancing contact that doesn't overwhelm with particulars but just totally inflames the imagination. So when Lusard, unseen by all those present and understood only by Claudine, kneels and kisses the hem of her dress – Lusard, a foreigner who belongs to little Denmark only through this symbolic act and through Claudine – this is the author's ingenious way of expressing the romantic character of Claudine's whole situation. If Lusard had taken her home to France as his bride, that would not have led to the same development in her as this romantic moment of contact, which is also the moment of parting. There are two things in one that a girl can demand in love if she demands all: that he is the beloved and that he has an Idea to give her into the bargain – then love's equation is absolute and complete.

All passion is rather like sailing: the wind must be strong enough to fill the sails, *uno tenore*, with one gust; there must not be too much tacking and going about before reaching deep water, nor too many preparations or too many ship's councils beforehand. It is a matter of passion gaining the power and authority to seize the unprepared in its almighty grasp. Thus Claudine stands alone with a world in her soul; then comes Lusard's hint to her. This is the romantic factor in the author's superbly planned situations. The power of infatuation is like the soaring of that winged steed[5] – it is entire in itself. But for everyday purposes! Then come prior knowledge, and circumstances, and considerations, and friends and relations, the trappings, the congratulators – audacity's triumphant enterprise is transformed into a bourgeois expedition: a carrier's wagon with all the passengers shouting 'Giddy-up', and love is the patient beast supposed to drag all this along. But not for Claudine. Bereft of any prior knowledge and thus deserving of the initiation, not one consideration occurs to her; for her, Lusard is the beloved and through him she is touched by an idea. This, from a romantic point of view, is initiation's supreme covenant.

This is how the beginning is arranged, but it is *still* a matter of the surroundings and circumstances again encouraging and psychologically supporting the romantic element. When two hefty fellows lead the snorting steed out for the race, what are they meant to do? They are meant to let go. Nothing else? That, after all, is easy enough. No, it is an art; they must know how to *let go with passion*; the slightest uncertainty or hesitation on their part will always hold the steed back a little; in letting go they must know precisely how to give it impetus. In pushing a boat off from the shore, the thing is to bend forward so as to add strength to the push and at the same time thrust oneself backwards to add to the impetus. As far as all passion is concerned, it is the case that all that the circumstances can do for one is to let go – with passion. But that is just how matters are arranged in W.'s house for Claudine, and the author's ingenuity may with reason demand what is even rarer than a cheerful giver and a happy worker, namely a joyful critic; that is, one who takes pleasure in seeing what the author has done. Merchant Waller is immersed in politics. And far from incommoding Claudine with curiosity and sympathy, the rather secretive nature of the quietly pondering Madame W. is more apt temptingly to encourage the young girl's secret love. Dalund spends his days absorbed in studying the expression of Madame W.'s mental states on her countenance (a study he continued as an old man by contemplating her portrait); but not the least inclined to track down other people's love affairs, he seems more in fear of the Frenchmen on account of his own relationship. Claudine is solitary and isolated, without the sympathy that brings congratulation as when one compliments a person who has found something by crying, 'Go halves!', and which often does make falling in love into something shared. Ferdinand W., the only one who suspects the love affair, is an enthusiastic troubadour for the Frenchmen and Lusard.

This is how *the love affair progresses*. The author knows how to arrange things in a way that puts the romantic factor in charge. But there is still what in the great poet's[6] words is the crucial thing needed to bring out their love: the possibility of their meeting alone. And even if something else is denied them – 'the moon shining through the branches of the beech tree in *springtime*' – the author thinks it is September that should really be called the month of love. In pushing a boat off from the shore, the thing is to bend forward so as to add strength to the push and at the same time thrust oneself backwards to add to the impetus – and when someone secretly in love, in greater peril than her beloved, already believes him killed in a duel, the reverse thrust of this thought of death is the most powerful impetus for love.

The wounded Lusard is brought to the Waller country house and the opportunity is thereby given to the lovers. Without a single preconceived idea or any guidance whatsoever, other than the eccentricity of love and of the age, with no confidant but love, Claudine becomes a sacrifice to her love. The psychological premisses adequately motivate her lapse, just as in turn they motivate her perseverance, for her lapse and her virtue are essentially the same romanticism.

Another question is whether the ideas of the age might not have made Claudine clearer about the step she had taken than she later proves to be. The way her later rather naïve ignorance about the consequences of her relationship with Lusard is depicted seems borrowed from another kind of romanticism, the pastoral–idyllic. Typical of the age of revolution would be for Claudine to come to realize that her relationship with Lusard was what was ordinarily called marriage, except for the relationship's natural side being emancipated from the ethically binding one, which was considered the antiquated aspect of marriage. Tender romanticism's all too innocent ignorance is least of all appropriate in the revolutionary age, standing out as something accidental in the context of a rendition of the reflection of the age of revolution. Lusard understands the matter more correctly, and accordingly in one of his lines calls her 'my little wife'.[7] Claudine, on the other hand, is more a girl led astray in a quite normal way by her love rather than by the influence of modern ideas. For although it is true that she hears Ferdinand Waller discussing these ideas, and he informs her of the relationship between Madame W. and Dalund, there is no indication of the impression this has made on her, how she has understood its implications for herself; on the contrary, she later proves to differ in no way from what is conventionally labelled a girl gone astray in romantic infatuation.

Lusard is the ardent, smooth, cultivated Frenchman, excitable in any mood including sadness, made in every respect for just such a relationship as this one with Claudine, except that his perseverance bears little relation to his easy mobility – that is, although it is not impossible for someone like this to behave as Lusard does, it would also be understandable if he behaved differently. Though psychologically one would have every right to be astonished if Claudine were to be untrue to herself, she herself would have found it even forgivable in Lusard had he been untrue to her, and she would still have gone on loving him.

Madame Waller has been the object of *Dalund's* love since she was quite young, but she misconstrued his silence and married while he was absent. Marriage has not improved her. Lacking inner contentment, 'she pursued only empty pleasures, found her highest bliss in being flirted with,* and regarded her appearance as the matter of most consequence' (cf. p. 37) – until the relationship with Dalund finally gives her refinement, a relationship to which Dalund considers himself to have a right, as his due, for so many years of fidelity and for a love such as his. Yet Madame W. is unable completely to master an inner voice that reminds her she is following a forbidden path, a voice that according to her own avowal becomes louder precisely because her improvement has let a light burst upon her that her neglected youth had failed to show her.† Meanwhile Dalund fights for the relationship even to the point of jealousy (for instance, of the Frenchmen), inspired as much by the formative and absolute influence he exerts by virtue of his masculine and personal superiority as by the ideas of his age.

Here again we have a difficulty. It is not in being seen to follow from, or in being borne out by, the idea of the age that the relationship between Madame W. and Dalund gives expression to that idea. Dalund champions the idea of the age in the relationship and consequently seeks to give new confirmation to an already existing relationship by securing for it the stamp of approval of the idea of the age. Purely personally, the relationship seems to have begun and to continue as the way in which these two have resolved a collision in their lives. The

---

* From this description one even becomes slightly confused about the age in which the scene happens.

† Were this collision carried to its extreme it would not be without psychological interest. She is improved by an illicit relationship and the improvement gives her insight into its illicitness. Suppose the improvement had triumphed in the victory of this superior insight so that because of it she gave up the relationship! That Madame W. is a self-contradiction is clear enough, moreover, the bringing out of which is due precisely to the author's psychological acuity. One is supposed neither to smile at the self-contradiction nor quickly to think it resolved just because it is perceived, still less hastily to condemn it. Indeed, when a man tells us he himself perceives what is reprehensible in his action and yet goes on doing it, let the ethical judge him and the aesthetic find him comical. With a woman it is somewhat different, especially where her strength can be seen in the very frailty of her devotedness. With Dalund she sees what is illicit in the relationship, but if she were without him she would not see it. Once femininely secure in a relationship that fills her whole soul, she can see that it is illicit. But if the relationship is broken off, the womanly needs in her will let her forget in erotic desperation that it was illicit.

difficulty, then, is that something seems to be missing in respect of the reciprocal transparency demanded by the novel's twofold task. The way the age is defined requires the middle term[8] of the individuality, the way the individuality is defined requires the middle term of the age, and the task of this transparency is to present novelistically a reflection of the age in domestic life. Or if one wanted to say that the author only seeks to show how people judged such a relationship in a revolutionary age, the rejoinder must be that the task is then a unique one, since the judgement consisted precisely in ignoring it; and also that Ferdinand W. is the only person who mentions it, and we learn nothing at all about how much the others know about it; and, finally, that the relationship itself indeed is presented. What is questionable in all this is surely that the author in the Preface appears to have set himself a third task – a comparison of the two ages.[9] Yet, superbly though the two Parts of the novel are arranged for the comparison, so, surely, should the author not have hinted at any such thing.

The remaining characters are less significant and do not lend themselves to special comment. Nor will I venture to mention or give examples of the many excellent details woven into the unfolding story: their presence is something we take for granted in the author of *A Story of Everyday Life*. One enjoys the reading, one doesn't give oneself critical airs by reviewing a novel like this stingily, as though it were the work of a beginner where the problem would be, as they say, to find at least 'something' to praise.

Were I, on the other hand, to point out in Part One what appears at least to me to be a less felicitous detail, I would name the baron and particularly his venture into the demonic, apart from which one might also ask whether he isn't limited to such a common type that the reflection of the age simply isn't to be detected there. A frivolous and in addition half-drunk baron, who in shrewish ill-temper gets the notion of killing little Charles, arouses neither horror nor interest – that is, the grudging interest characteristic of the ambiguity of the demonic. He fails to arouse fear, because with a drunken man one's first thought is that it will pass; and he fails to arouse interest, partly because he is drunk and partly because his frivolity is anything but masculine. Nor must it be made to look as though he terrified Claudine, for although this sort of thing may make him vile and disgusting in her eyes, it is not terrifying. And what is the psychological motivation for this strange episode? Even if we assume that once the possibility of a relationship with Claudine has been shattered, the baron reverts to his old ways, which only she would have the power to bend to the obedience of love, does it then follow that he can continue carrying on in this way? After all, he was originally good-natured, bore the outward marks of good breeding, and Claudine's influence on him, even at such a moment, must have some psychological effect. To me the situation seems unbecoming and not really authentic either.

Now to Part Two. *Mariane*. Roused unfairly and all too early from youthful illusion and driven into the painful reality of pressing household tasks, vexed by daily insults, she humbly works out the bitter problem of being more or less a housemaid in her own parents' house. All the haughty disdain and, on the other hand, foppish familiarities to which such a servant can be subjected are no strangers to her. And the bitterness is the greater that she is not only defenceless but has been thrown to the wolves – because she is the daughter. On the other hand, she very early gets into the habit of perfecting an incorruptible nature of quiet inwardness; she is particularly trained in preserving a secret understanding, since the whole reality of her circumstances is only a vexatious meaninglessness, for even with her father in her father's house she maintains, *qua* daughter, a merely secret understanding, where only in the hall or in passing, or when no one can see them, dare the father speak to her in a fatherly way – in the way lovers who lack their parents' consent contrive to see each other, to talk to each other in the hall when the parents in the living-room officially oppose the association. Were Mariane in love she would be forced to make a secret of it, or else it would be the signal for a new maltreatment: should someone love Miss Maren, should anyone want a 'little slut' like that, as her stepmother calls her,[10] she would be liable to lose her position with the commercial counsellor's lady, just so they'd be rid of this love nonsense.

And Mariane *is* in love. We will now follow the features of the author's excellently constructed situation in order to explain her psychologically. These couldn't be called harmful at the level of chatty sympathy, but neither are they favourable. They do not let go with passion, neither do they restrain by misconceived kindness and concern, yet they do vexingly exert restraint. No doubt it is true that the life of love is inwardness, and that inwardness is in itself just what it is and therefore may be the same whether, for instance, we are dealing with someone who goes out on a balcony to gaze at the starlit night or with a prisoner doing a life sentence who through a crevice steals a glance at a single star – though the latter's inwardness is perhaps the greater; yet the point with love, just as with human birth, is nevertheless that the condition of things, the surroundings, exert their psychological predisposition, have a great influence on what transpires. Mariane wanted with the same inwardness as Claudine to be true to herself, and yet her love differed essentially in all eternity from Claudine's.

Being in love is the culmination of a person's purely human existence, which is a double existence, and for that reason it is at the same time just as much inwardness as a relationship outwards, towards actual life. Equilibrium in the relationship is happy love. Less inwardness and a preponderance in the relationship towards the actual is a less beautiful love; a preponderance of inwardness and less of a relationship to the actual tends towards unhappy love.

So it is with Mariane; she has become all too well acquainted with the misery of actual life, and the surroundings impress their vexations upon her daily. Instead of love's victorious, all-conquering courage that, convinced in its enthusiastic ignorance that reality is the world where love has its home, dares in matters of love to demand everything of actual life – instead of that, she has something of love's inner sadness. The inwardness can amount to the same thing, just as a retreat may be as great an achievement as the most brilliant victory, but the difference is essential. Instead of sensing her love as a vocation emanating from a world that wants compliance in all things, she has accustomed herself in her inwardness to comply in renunciation: her love is at the same instant in secret acquiescence with the fact that it, too, will become a repressed inwardness, a hidden life others know nothing of, and which will be at one and the same time a higher state of health and yet, speaking humanly, an infirmity. The inwardness can amount to the same thing, as it is an equally difficult task to die as to live. Inwardness is the real pearl, which is formed, as is known, inside the oyster by the absorption of dew. But according to an ancient author[11] it is supposed to make a difference whether it is morning or evening dew; so too it makes a difference whether the genuine individuality of the love is formed with hope or with remembrance.

As with all passion, so with love: the one who receives the initiation is *unimpeded* in the initiated moment of falling in love, *unobstructed* on the foolhardy summit of illusion, freely and infinitely surveying the whole world; there must be no paltry sympathy, but also no teases that keep the light-armed one from scaling the dizzy heights, and who in that moment prevent the unimpeded one from catching the view. If everything is to turn out well, this protected moment must not be denied, this moment when all existence, enchanted, obeys every beck and call, when nothing, *nothing*, lessens love's unbounded abandonment in illusion; and this is something other than all the lovers' caresses and occurs *privatissime*, since it is the presupposition that unites the lovers, the precipitator, infinity's advance payment on which they must live the many or the few years. This Mariane lacks.

The author has depicted all this superbly; and it is important for the relationship between Mariane and Bergland, seeing that it psychologically motivates, on her side too, the possibility of separation through fear of financial embarrassment. Mariane has none of love's jubilant rapture to counterpose to Bergland's discouragement; she does not have love's triumphant courage to take feminine charge of the holy expedition of marriage when the beloved loses his composure. Psychologically, it would not be devoid of interest to imagine the relationship along those lines, although it would defeat the novel's aim, which also has to do with the age. The author has understood this very well. Mariane is unable to muster any resistance; she herself is affected by a troubled reflection, and in her lines resounds a sad familiarity with actuality, a resignation regarding love itself and its claims to universal validity. But the inwardness is still there, just as eternal, and as life-long, as in the most rapturous infatuation, essentially as strong but differing essentially in its expression. Even if she is willing to give up Bergland, she will not take back her ring because she will not give up the love. 'Neither will I give back yours. Like my love I have carried it secretly for three years, I will not give it up in the years left to me.'[12] Here she is at her most sublime, yet the love is not a beckoning but a withdrawal into inwardness. Marked 'by the quiet virtues',[13] her love's inwardness is that of a girl who dedicates herself to suffering. She has suffered much from the actual world, but this blow seems decisive. So also Caesar remained erect when the conspirators plunged their daggers into him, but on seeing that Brutus was a party to it, he wrapped himself in his cloak and gave himself up to death with these words: 'You too, Brutus, my son!'[14] Troubled by reflection, the greatest resistance Mariane can muster against Bergland's passion, in the passionate tension of impatience, is the provisional 'that she will patiently wait' (cf. p. 269), but even this resistance is in keeping with reflection.

How well arranged everything is here! The psychological portrait and the reflection of the age. The good, in the strident heyday of a jack-of-all-trades superficiality, must lead a cowed and clandestine life, in an *ecclesia pressa*,[15] as Mariane does. On the other hand, in an age given to reflecting, even this deep intensity may not remain altogether untouched by reflection, even in relation to the one thing it possesses, an infatuation. A spontaneous, enthusiastic lover in Mariane's position would consider Bergland mad; she would be utterly unable for the life of her to understand his financial worries; but neither would such another lover be able in the least to understand Mariane's resignation. Such a situation could only be humorous and Bergland an essentially comic figure, representing as he does a rather prosaic point of view.

Ferdinand Bergland is an eccentric fellow who has lost his way along possibility's bold antecedent in life, who has included a love affair in the multiplicity of his plans and studies, and is now about to run aground on the consequent.[16] A marriage, which for him should be the hyphen, assumes a fearsome shape and he becomes diffident – a desperate once-for-all decision has to take the place of action and the continuity of an essential passion. The seeming strength involved in making the decision is really only the expression of impotence, and the reason he gives is therefore basically incidental. He could just as well have mentioned any other reason, because the real reason is the disproportion between possibility and actuality, which now grabs at this detail as though it were the reason. His desperate decision, and the action it gives rise to, are therefore meaningless – and a decision and action which, if things went as he wanted, would have essentially amounted to nothing. Deciding not to will to do this or that, neither more nor less than not willing in itself, is really deciding to become nothing. Unless the person deciding not to will enters at that very moment into the service of a higher idea, his decision and action are empty. It is this that determines the outcome of life's collisions, and decides if the passion is justified or not. Ferdinand by making his decision has become essentially no clearer about himself than before, but has merely retreated headlong into darkness about himself; all he does is *referre pedem*,[17] and in terms of the ideality of his own personality, in stepping backward there is no step forward. His worries about making a living, in that form, do not constitute a real view of existence; but anyone who takes it upon himself to manage, or at least disturb, another's life on the scale that Ferdinand did, even though from an ethical point of view the intervention will always be a mistake, must at least have understood himself in the light of a more essential view of existence, in the light of an Idea to which his life can relate – precisely, when he breaks with Mariane.

How well arranged everything is here, too: the psychological portrait and the reflection of the age. In another age it might have ended with Mariane's patience gaining at least an interim – until Ferdinand's worries were dispelled. But from an inward and a romantic standpoint our own age, despite all its plans and anticipations and pronouncements and presuppositions, is essentially without passion. This is precisely why a sudden expression of despair appears again in a desperate action or decision, an alternation which is the lawless law for the extremes in such a way of life.

Mrs Waller, the commercial counsellor's lady. If one might speak in the same way of composite human beings as one does in distinguishing between noble and base metal and those having something in between called 'plated', a composite that can be deceptive, then the lady of the house would be aptly so called. She has a plated virtuosity in being anything you like: at one moment charming and the next almost repulsive; lovable and yet tiresome in her bustling self-importance, decorative yet making a virtual exhibition of herself in her gilded attire, demure yet dallying, cultured and yet painful to the genuinely cultured, shrewd about life yet almost mindless, flirtatious from beginning to end. Her characterization cannot be anything other than this variegated description, because there is nothing essential in her and her out-wardness must be described by enumerating items. The ostentatious virtuosity is consummated and turns back into itself in the smug conceit that she is what a woman of the world should be, which is why she proudly and calmly dares anything on the strength of her reputation. And yet her nature is in a profound sense equivocal, for as one of the Apostles (James) more or less puts it: purity of heart is to will one thing.[18] Even Madame W. in Part One is in a way less equivocal.

The mastery with which the author handles such a glittering and grotesque frailty is admirable, always conveying the impression of a fictitiously real character; likewise the ease with which the combinations of situation are invented, the naturalness with which the thread of continuity runs through the story,* constantly throwing light on the lady's lack of character in the passing mirror of reflection, but fleetingly, for there is in fact nothing to dwell upon; yes, there must be no

---

* Thus, to cite just one example, the scene in the commercial counsellor's house when Lusard, tired of listening to the lady of the house's bravura piano-playing, retires to the study to talk with Counsellor Dalund. A wistful agreeableness now pervades the two reminiscers talking about the past – until Arnold, the music having stopped towards the end of their conversation, sits down behind the open door and unsuspectingly overhears them, whereupon the lady herself and the equerry enter – and the conversation of the present age begins. Such realism. I don't believe the most hard-to-please critic could find anything to displease him here – certainly no objection to the effect that anything happening before one's eyes here wasn't as if one saw it oneself. And yet what ingenuity in the plot, to bring the two ages together in this way! The past is living and being relived in remembrance in the intimacy of the study, and out in the drawing-room, which is the encircling frame, the present age is strident, yes, is even in its exhibitionist brash-ness on the point of publicizing the secrets of the study. Just as the best horseman is said to guide his snorting steed with a thread, making it look as if the horse with its enormous strength has the upper hand when in fact this impression, far more than just that, is precisely the expression of the rider's absolute control, so also the author guides the forward movement of the situation so naturally that, although there seems to be no design, this appearance is precisely the expression of the omnipresent purpose, which only shows itself by concealing itself.

dwelling, for then Mrs Waller becomes someone else. The art lies in the fact that the presentation contains the repetition of the psychological construal, and just as the dallying demonstrates the unstable emptiness, so the wife throughout the novel is in a state of unstable bustle, shown in this transitory relation to older and younger men, to her own children, to her husband, to Mariane, to the maid. Especially superb is the proportioning of the relationships between the five female characters: the wife's demonstrative maternalism in relation to the two little darlings who are already trained to be 'respecters of persons', the parody in Colette's copying her mother, which has perhaps contributed to the mother's becoming bored with her,* and finally, the profound satire upon the wife implicit in Mariane's quiet nature.

If in describing a person's essential nature one recalls Pliny's famous words, *omnia ad conscientiam, nil ad ostentationem*,[19] one need only reverse those words (*omnia ad ostentationem, nil ad conscientiam*) and you have a description of this lady's nature, which is to be the inside out, or a contrary being. But to be reminded once again, as it befits a critic to be true to the richness in the author's portrayal: it takes far more skill to present such a character than to describe a person with an essence. Some may even find my remarks about this character quite suggestive. Yes, these days it isn't unthinkable that someone be stupid enough to find my account in its brevity more exhaustive than the author's. This, alas, is a great misunderstanding people have come by only in our declamatory age, and by doing so they do disservice to every work of art. For there is an infinite leap from this brevity to the trick of being able to present such a character. Criticism in our time is like so many people – it is constantly letting itself be duped by abstract possibility and foreshortened perspective, which are anything but creative, and by great projects and summary surveys, which are anything but fruitful. No, whatever one thinks about presenting an age in a feminine figure like this, one thing is certain: the character is a masterpiece of the portrayal of triviality, a masterpiece all the way down to the most trivial detail, yes, to the tip of the rosy tongue she sticks out at her

---

* For what is essential and true may be possessed by several persons simultaneously, but affectation is always domineering and envious.

husband – a quick and secret response to an unspoken accusation (p. 216).

Counsellor Dalund. A venerable old man is in himself pleasant to behold, but Dalund has the added interest for the reader that we know him from the days of his youth. Of course, any biography can in a sense produce the same effect; but only in a sense, for it produces no illusion as the novel does, letting us become contemporary with Dalund not just straightforwardly, young then old, but making him our contemporary in two different eras.

But does the character remain psychologically consistent? Undoubtedly. But where does the satirical trait that was not really noticeable in his youth, and which the author didn't allow to come out either, come from? In Part One he is basically the young commonsensical man with the intelligent face, the talented lawyer who will not allow himself to be carried away by factions, even though the divisive power crucially estranging people from one another in heated partisanship is a world-historical event. He retains his equilibrium, mainly level-headed and rhapsodic only in his relation to Madame Waller. Now, good sense, neutrality and legal acuteness are essential to a satirist; but it doesn't follow that wherever these elements are present there is a satirist. Times, however, have changed, and have changed him a little likewise. There is a psychological consistency in the fact that in this change he should become satirical. Neutrality is really only conceivable when the factions are of some significance, when it is truly an idea that separates them. If, however, the times are without significance, and the factional disagreement a kind of theatrical pretence of merely playing at revolution, then the person who in the time of the upheavals was neutral will become a satirist. Neutrality consists in a positive recognition of the respective validity, *valore intrinseco*,[20] of each of the factions. Take away this pre-condition of the relation of neutrality and *eo ipso* the neutrality is negatively qualified as satire, because to be neutral with regard to a chimerical either/or means *either* one is a fool, since the neutrality is just as foolish as the trifling parties in relation to which it negatively defines itself, and so it is a possibility only for a trifling person; *or*, by essentially being something, one is *eo ipso* satirical. The man is, then, essentially the same: the change is merely a reflection of the change in the times.

Dalund has also mellowed.* This too is quite as it should be, and not just because it is the reward that a gifted man has coming to him in his old age, while only a person of less consequence gets peevish when elderly. But isn't this too a reflection of the changing times? He feels exceptional, this old man stricken in years yet who belonged to a more significant age, and essentially does belong to it – it is exactly this that is the mellowing factor, the firmness of bearing that makes him gentle through the secret communication of remembrance with the past. As an old man he belongs in the passage of time to two ages. He is thus bifrontal: mellow when he looks back, and on turning towards the present age a little satirical – for everyday purposes the lovable old man. He is not dull in his mind, and perhaps also because he still has something to fight for, since the love affair lives on in his soul, he battles still with the enemy – the uncertainty of illicit possession – and against doubt: the question is whether fidelity does indeed atone for guilt, whether fidelity might win for him a reunion with his heart's desire. For just as once Madame Waller's lawful husband stood in the way, now eternity might seem to be doing the same thing.

Charles Lusard. The novel is two ages. The two Parts are distinct, and yet there is still a connecting link, a transition that ingeniously joins them. This is the figure of Charles Lusard. He doesn't belong to the past, he is too young for that, and he is not entirely unaffected by the reflectiveness of the present age. His is a personality that has remained constant, and here again we have the unity of psychological outlook and a reflection of the age. His childhood impressions and, later, the singular ceremoniousness that hovered over his parents' domestic life must naturally arouse a certain wistful rhapsodizing in his soul, which has quite naturally been exhausted in foreign travels and in a conscious striving that has failed to bring him into a personal relationship with anyone, whatever youthful cravings his soul harboured, precisely because his wistful side had an isolating effect.

This is how a rhapsodic reserve splits a young man's soul. The youth's need for comradeship goes unfelt because already he is living

---

* This shows, too, that the satire in him is not to be confused with any bitterness in the aged.

in remembrance. Not even love's season has a chance, since he is already betrothed in inwardness. The solitary youth's outwardly directed endeavours are aimed at external enterprises that can keep him busy without his getting essentially involved with anyone, without his missing anyone – precisely because in remembrance he does miss someone. In this fashion he has travelled both in the Old World and the New, and then returned to his estate. His is an individuality that has, that is to say, stayed constant. But this also calls for an element of reflection and of self-reflection, and this again is, on the other hand, a reflection of the age, which, itself indecisive, has not had the power over him to sweep him along. So really he belongs to neither age. The idea he represents – having renounced his own life in order to make a few people happy – doesn't really belong to either of them. Charles Lusard, precisely through being constant, is the transition. In a revolutionary age an individual of this kind would no doubt become partisan; in the present age he may not have attained the harmonious and thoroughly cultured equilibrium that distinguishes his noble and independent bearing, even though his soul follows pensively on the heels of a memory. For an unhappy individual (as we must call someone whom no contemporary age or life-situation motivates for the future), he is happy, but his is still not a happy individuality.

What is amazing about this novel is that everything is so true to the category,[21] while when in reading it the whole seems so unpretentious that the cursory reader – if he should happen to see this review – might be taken aback and think I find more in it than there is to be found, etc. Alas, I cannot accept that reader's compliment but must pass it on to the proper person, the author, who even if I had understood it all is still, after all, first the inventor and then, secondly, also the one who with his art could again conceal it; and, finally, is perhaps privy to much in the novel that I have not been able to discover.

There is still another character in Part Two of the novel: *Johannes Milner*, the overseer of the estate, a jovial man who after a discouraging career crisis, without livelihood and suspected of an unstable temperament, found a position with Lusard that made him a happy man. In the owner's absence he has managed the estate with care and wisdom, and now in his healthy joy in life occasionally entertains the wish to see

Lusard settled in marriage. That Johannes Milner has been very active on the estate is clear, but in the novel he seems fairly unoccupied. Yet a friendship such as that between Milner and Lusard is not unimportant in throwing light on Lusard. Just such a friendship throws his loneliness into relief. It is not the unanimity of two like-minded people, nor attachment's urge for the other's confidence. Though so mollified and satisfied with life, with himself, his comforts and his marriage, Milner nevertheless finds something extinct and ruined, something that makes him sad to behold,[22] in Lusard's long trips abroad 'all by himself'. Add to this the fact that Lusard is Milner's benefactor, and however careful that noble, cultured man is about toning down any echo of disharmony in that relationship, it is still there, reinforcing the solitary one's superiority and, again, distance.

It wouldn't occur to me to cite examples of details in the second Part, because the details here are *all* totally significant. Just a single line of Lusard's grated, on me at least, because I thought it unsuitable in his mouth when said to a lady.[23] What he said may be altogether true; its questionableness lies in its relation to the speaker and the speaker's situation.

III The Results of Observing the Two Ages

So here I am now at the final section, and with the difficulty the author has posed the critic by himself making as if to offer a criticism. Would the author had not done that! I say this not for my own sake, certainly, since in another respect I am happy to take the hints offered, though I shall not copy them and pass the criticism off as my own. But I think the book is the worse for that Preface, precisely because it makes it possible for quick minds and loose tongues to say straight away, 'Is that all?' – 'That can be said in a page.' Well, of course, it makes no difference at all what a voluble person says, or an impudent and naughty child. But all the same, with regard to a book with a literary signature distinguished by its honour and dignity, it is clear there is something even more to be desired, something we who are perhaps all too used to malice almost forget: that the voluble person or the naughty child simply keep quiet. What seems unimportant when it happens to others appears a significant incongruity when it happens to the exalted; and what seems bearable when it happens to oneself distresses one when it happens to the distinguished. When, because of the muddy going, a person has pulled on his rubber boots, he sets off with confidence. But if, just then, he sees a young girl, say, who has resolved without a single splash the difficult task of negotiating the not so very short way from her home, happily aware of the lightness of her own gliding gait – and then along comes some oaf who splatters her in passing, it pains him. It seems to him an injustice on the part of life to lump the heterogeneous together in time, it discomfits him that the street is for everybody instead of everybody getting out of the young girl's way – and in Danish literature at present there is no right of way, and absolutely no police who might at least keep the pavements clear of labourers for hire, porters and louts.

The Age of Revolution

It's not a question here of an ethico-philosophical assessment of [the age's] validity, but of the consequences of its special character as this is reflected, and the task is to suggest such consequences only at the level of generality corresponding to the details of the author's novelistic account.

The age of revolution is essentially passionate, for which reason it essentially possesses *form*. Even the most vehement utterance of an essential passion has *eo ipso* form, for that is the expression itself, and therefore it has in its form, again, an apology, something conciliatory. Only in the service of an altogether outward and indifferent dialectic is the form not the content's *own* other, and thereby the content itself, but an irrelevant third something. Any written correspondence, for instance, that bears the mark of inwardness in the expression of real feeling has *eo ipso* form. But whether the letter is folded shapelessly is something only the altogether external dialectic could, with specious solemnity, be made to treat as a question of form.

The age of revolution is essentially passionate, for which reason it essentially possesses *culture*. For the degree of essential culture is the resilience of inwardness.* A maidservant genuinely in love is essentially cultured; a common man with his mind vigorously and passionately made up is essentially cultured. Outward, piecemeal dressage in relation to an inner emptiness, the strutting extravagance of weeds compared to the meek bending of the blessed corn, the mechanical counting of the beat in relation to the lacklustre dance, the painstaking decoration of the binding in relation to the book's deficiency – all this, simply as form, is affectation. In laying stress on the cultured in the first age, the novel operates also with an accidental extra, to be sure, in so far as the age of revolution is represented in Copenhagen by a remarkable small band of remarkably cultured Frenchmen.

The age of revolution is essentially passionate, for which reason it must be able to be violent, uncurbed, wild, ruthless towards everything but its idea. But *rawness* is something it is less liable to be accused of, precisely because it has at least a purpose. A person who, however much his striving is outwardly directed, is essentially turned inward owing to an essential passion that relates to an idea, is never raw. A hurricane, an earthquake, the raging elements are not what, weather-wise, one refers to as 'raw'; to define that you would have to say, 'It's the cheerless lack of character.' So too in the world of individuals: remove the essential passion, the one purpose, then everything becomes an insignificant featureless outwardness; the flowing current of ideality stops and the life that people share becomes a stagnant lake – and that is rawness.

---

* The author of *A Story of Everyday Life*, with his noble humanity, has been frequently aware of this, and in this novel, too, has with a few strokes intimated such a character in Mrs Lyng, the sea-captain's widow. 'She had gone through a great deal in life and was one of those people never adequately appreciated, in whose heart kindness and gentleness take the place of upbringing and education, whom memory of the sufferings and injustices they have undergone teaches gentility in company regardless of any outward station in life' (p. 87).

Purely dialectically – and let us work them out dialectically without regard to any specific age – the relations are as follows. When the individuals (severally) relate essentially and passionately to an idea and, on top of that, in union essentially relate to the same idea, that relation is perfect and normal. The relation singles out individually (each has himself for himself) and unites ideally. In the essential inward directedness there is that modest reticence between man and man that prevents crude presumption. In the relation of unanimity to the idea is the elevation that again forgets the accident of the particulars in consideration of the whole. Thus individuals never come too close to each other in a brute sense, just because they are united at an ideal distance. The unanimity of the singled-out is the band playing well orchestrated music. If, on the other hand, individuals relate to an idea merely en masse (that is, without the individual, inward-directed singling out), we get violence, unruliness, unbridledness; but if there is no idea for the individuals en masse, nor any individually singling-out inward-directedness, then we have rawness. The harmony of the spheres is the unity of each planet relating to itself and to the whole. Remove one of the relations and there will be chaos. But in the world of individuals the relation is not the only constituting factor, and so there are two forms. Remove the relation to oneself, and we have the mass's tumultuous relating to an idea; but remove this too, and we have rawness. People then push and shove, and rub up against each other in futile outwardness. There is none of that modesty of inwardness that decently distances the one from the other. There is then a stir and a commotion that end in nothing. No one has anything for himself and united they possess nothing either, so they become vexed and squabble with one another. Then, it is not even those songs of joyful conviviality that unite friends; then, it is not those dithyrambic songs of revolt that collect the crowds; then, it is not the sublime rhythm of religious fervour that under divine surveillance musters the countless generations to review before the heavenly hosts.

No, gossip and rumour and specious importance and apathetic envy become a surrogate for both this and that. Individuals do not turn in inwardness towards themselves and away from each other, nor outwards in unanimity over an idea, but towards each other in crippling and disheartened, tactless, levelling reciprocity. The idea passage is blocked. The individuals are at cross-purposes with themselves and each other, the selfish and the mutually reflected opposition is like a quagmire – and now one is sitting in it. In joy's stead steps a kind of whimpering discontent, in sorrow's stead a kind of stubborn, surly staying-power, in enthusiasm's stead a loquacious worldly wisdom. But it is one thing to save one's life by casting the spell of a story, as in *A Thousand and One Nights*, another to debar oneself from the spell of enthusiasm over an idea and the rebirth of passion, by being loquacious. Suppose such an age invented the swiftest means of transport and communication, unlimited ways of managing combined financial resources; how ironic that the rapidity of the transport system and the speed of the communication stand in inverse relation to the dilatoriness of indecision. The superiority of a prudence that boasts of not letting itself be carried away (which can be quite all right if one is sitting in a quagmire) is a somewhat plebeian invention.

The age of revolution is essentially passionate, for which reason it also has a concept of *decorum*. It could well have a false concept of decorum, but it does not lack the concept. One would think decorum was a category of the understanding, yet it is anything but. In this it is like the distinction between verse and prose. One would think the lyric had to be quite unconstrained, yet it is precisely the lyric that is bound, though the stanza itself is not an invention of a tight-laced understanding; on the contrary, it is the lyric's own happy invention. Similarly with decorum. It is feeling's and passion's own invention, and just as prose is unconstrained speech, so prosiness is an unconcern that does not know a decorum. It is not lack of restraint that brings about that awful result, but dismal lack of character. The essential passion is in the last resort its own guarantee that there is something sacred, and it is this that gives rise to the determinant: decorum. Not even idolatry, when passion is essentially present in the pagan, is devoid of godliness; he has the concept that God is to be feared even if his concept is a false one. But prosiness lacks a concept. In the same way, if the age of revolution tolerates a relationship with a married woman, in spite of this being a false concept of decorum it does have such a concept. The permissibility of the relationship, reflected in its impermissibility, is therefore expressed by the requirement that the relationship be secret. This secrecy in turn indicates that the relationship, essentially one of passion under the seal of silence, gratifies the two parties. Remove the passion and the decorum too disappears, in which case the relationship probably does not get going, but then people talk about it. So even if the age of revolution wanted to abolish the form of marriage, it wouldn't have abolished the intrinsic value of falling in love, for the very reason that where there is an essential passion there is also a decorum.

The age of revolution is essentially passionate and to that extent has immediacy; and yet its immediacy is not the first immediacy, and in the highest sense it is no final immediacy either but an *immediacy of reaction* and to that extent *provisional*. The latter is decisive with respect to the endurance of this passion. It may well be that in actual life any number may remain to the end true to themselves in the passion, but in terms of the idea it must end with the single individual being untrue to himself because it is a provisional idea. In terms of the idea, it is only in the highest idea, which is the religious, that a person can find definitive rest; on the other hand, it may well be that many remain true to themselves in the provisional all their lives.* The revolutionary age's immediacy is a restoring of natural conditions, as opposed to a fossilized formalism which by losing the originary character of the ethical has become a wizened ruination, a petty-minded custom and practice. Precisely as reaction, it can be transformed by a single deviation into untruth, which in an accidental manner accentuates the polemical, as if it came to the point of love being love only when it is adultery.

In the novel, the reactionary immediacy of the age of revolution is captured in its reflection in domestic life. It is reflected in the relationship between Madame Waller and Dalund, in that between father and son (Counsellor of Justice Waller and Ferdinand Waller); it is reflected in the political view that resonates in the dialogue and in the conversation. It wants, in the relation between father and son, in a reactionary manner to do away with the inexplicables of piety and to make nature the

---

* Lusard remains true to himself in the idea, though with the qualification that he is enthusiastic about Napoleon, will even fight for him. Ferdinand Waller is personally changed and admits to Claudine that it was she who remained true to the idea.

only determinant of the relationship: thus dependency is abolished on attaining majority, when one's parents should be one's equals and friends. Neither this idea, nor indeed even that of freedom and equality, constitutes lack of form so long as the idea itself is the truth essentially enthusing the enthusiasts, for inwardness is not abolished. It by no means indicates lack of form when the religious idea inspires a brotherhood to make being brothers and sisters an expression of equality, for uniformity is the essential form; nor is it any empty abstraction so long as inwardness inheres. Formlessness is simply absence of content. Thus if a woman in a fit of boredom were to get the idea of adorning herself and dressing up gorgeously, this would be lack of form for the simple reason that there would be no idea behind it. The naked Archimedes is adorned with joy over his discovery and is therefore in effect really dressed.[1] One must bear this in mind particularly in our day and age when, for instance, skill with form is on the point of becoming formless simply because nothing has essential meaning and everything so little meaning.

The age of revolution is essentially passionate, for which reason it is essentially *revelation*, revelation by a manifestation of strength that is unquestionably a definite something and does not change perfidiously with the aid of a conjectural criticism concerning what it is the age really wants.

The age of revolution is essentially passionate, for which reason it has *not annulled the principle of contradiction* and can become either good or evil; and whichever path is chosen, the *impetus* of passion is such as must be discernible – the footprint of a deed must mark its progress or its deviation. A decision has to be arrived at, but this again is the saving factor, for decision is the little magic word that existence respects. If, on the other hand, the individual will not act, then existence cannot help. To be like that king, Agrippa,[2] on the point of believing or of acting, is the most exhausting state imaginable if one stays in it for long. Claudine goes astray; the *impetus* of passion marks the decision but supports her again. Her *plerophoria eis pathos*[3] topples but also strengthens her. One cannot accuse an age that is very reflective of being powerless, just like that and with no further ado, for there may be much power, but it goes to waste in the futility of reflection. With some illusion as support, it takes far less effort to achieve at least something than when all illusion is lost. And just as scurvy is cured by eating vegetables, perhaps a person worn out in reflection needs not so much strength as a little illusion.

It is not unusual to hear someone, confused about what to do in a certain situation, complain about the special nature of the case in hand and claim that one can safely act if the situation is a great event of the kind where there is only an either/or. This is a misapprehension and an illusion of the understanding. There is no such case. The presence of the crucial either/or lies in the individual's own impassioned desire to act decisively, in his own competence. And a competent man longs for an either/or in every case because he won't have more. Once the individual no longer has essential enthusiasm in his passion, on the other hand, but is spoiled by letting his understanding thwart him every time he is about to act, he never in his life comes to discover the disjunction. And even if his intellect, in its probing resourcefulness, be adequate for an entire household, he has still not understood his life in anticipation or in the moment of action; and it cannot be understood afterwards either, since essentially the action did not take place, and the coherence of his life became a loquacious continuation or a continued loquacity, a participial or infinitive phrase in which the subject has to be understood, or rather isn't to be found at all, because it can by no means be construed from the meaning, as the grammarians say, for meaning is just what it lacks. The whole thing becomes a flux made up of a little bit of resolution and a little bit of situation, a little bit of prudence and a little bit of courage, a little bit of probability and a little bit of faith, a little bit of action and a little bit of event. Anyone who has perpetrated the swindle of gaining abnormally good sense at the cost of the capacity to will and the passion to act, is strongly disposed on that account to stiffen his spinelessness with miscellaneous deliberations beforehand which feel their way ahead, and with various deliberations afterwards that re-explain what happened. Compared with this, an action is some brief something or other, and to all appearances some poor something or other, yet in truth it is something definite. The other is more splendid, but a brilliant misery.

When a Roman emperor sits at the table surrounded by guards, it is a magnificent spectacle, but if the reason is fear the grandeur pales. So, too, when the individual dare not stand tight-lipped by his word, does not stand boldly and openly on the pedestal of a conscious act, but is surrounded by a host of considerations before and after that make it impossible for him to catch sight of the action. Just as an elderly man puts his hand to his back in support and leans on a cane, so abnormal good sense supports itself with a reflection in advance and comes to its own aid afterwards, with re-explanatory reflection – and why? Just because no action took place. Instead of that child of a god, the silent terse decision, the generation gives birth to a changeling of the understanding that has everything at its fingertips.

The Present Age

The aim as I see it, considered at a fairly general level and in the critical service of the novel, is here again to bring out just those specific elements depicted with such novelistic skill by the author.

The present age is essentially *sensible, reflective, dispassionate, eruptive in its fleeting enthusiasms and prudently indolent in its relaxation.*

If we had figures for the consumption of prudence from generation to generation as we do for the consumption of spirits, etc., we would be amazed to see what vast quantities are consumed nowadays, what amounts of reflection and deliberation and consideration even a small private family gets through despite its ample income, what amounts even children and young people consume; for just as the children's crusade[4] typifies the Middle Ages, so child intelligence typifies the present age. Is there anyone who makes even just one tremendous blunder any more? Nowadays not even a suicide does away with himself in desperation, but considers this step so long and so sensibly that he is strangled by good sense, casting doubt on whether he may really be called a suicide, seeing that it was mainly consideration that took his life. A premeditated suicide he was not – rather, a suicide by premeditation. It would be the hardest of tasks to be a prosecuting counsel in a time like this, since the whole generation has legal competence and its skill, its good sense, its virtuosity consist in letting matters reach a verdict and a decision without ever acting.

If we say of a revolutionary age that it *takes a wrong turn*, then we may say of the present age that it *turns out badly*.[5] The individual and the generation are constantly at cross-purposes with themselves and with each other and it would be impossible for a prosecuting counsel to establish any fact, just because there is none. From abundant presumptive evidence one might conclude that something extraordinary has occurred, or is just about to, but the inference would be mistaken, for the evidence itself is all there is to the present age's sole attempt at a show of strength; and its ingenuity and virtuosity in contriving captivating illusions, the fleeting nature of its eruptive enthusiasms, aided by the deceptive shortcut of schemes for formal changes, rate as highly in respect of calculating shrewdness and the negative use of power as the age of revolution's achievements in respect of energetic and transformative passion. Exhausted by its chimerical exertions, the present age then relaxes for a while in complete indolence. Its condition is like that of the sleepyhead in the morning: big dreams, then torpor, then hitting on a witty or clever excuse for staying in bed.

The single individual (however well intentioned many a such may be, however much energy they might possibly have if only they could come to use it) has not bottled up passion enough in himself to tear free of the net of reflection and of reflection's seductive uncertainty. The surroundings, contemporaneity, possess neither incident nor united passion, but in a negative union create a reflected opposition that first, for a moment, makes play with unreal prospects, and then gives the illusion of strength through a brilliant evasion,[6] namely that one has done the wisest thing after all, by refraining from taking any action. *Vis inertia*[7] is the basis of the age's tergiversation,[8] and every passionless person congratulates himself on being the original inventor – and becomes even cleverer. In the age of revolution weapons were freely distributed, and during the crusades the emblem of the enterprise was conferred publicly. Similarly today, we are treated freely to rules of prudence, computations of considerations, etc. If we could assume that a whole generation had the diplomatic task of keeping time at bay, so that anything at all was continually prevented from happening yet all the time it seemed as though something *were* happening, then our age would unquestionably be achieving something just as prodigious as the age of revolution. Were someone to try the experiment of forgetting all he knew about the age, and the factual relativities by which habit so excites our expectations, and arrive as though from another world and read some book or other, a newspaper article, or just talk to a passer-by, the impression he got would be: My God, something must be going to happen this evening – or else something must have happened the night before last!

As against the age of revolution, which acted, the present age is the age of advertisement, the age of miscellaneous announcements: nothing happens, but what does happen is instant notification. An uprising in the present age is the most unthinkable of all; such a *show of energy* would strike the calculating sensibleness of the age as ludicrous. A political virtuoso, on the other hand, might be able to perform a *feat of artistry* that was amazing in quite another way. He could word an invitation, proposing a general meeting for the purpose of deciding on a revolution, so carefully that even the censor would have to pass it. And then on the evening in question he could give the gathering an impression so deceptive that it seemed as though they had achieved the uprising; whereupon they would disperse quite peacefully, having spent a very pleasant evening. Acquiring enormously solid learning would be practically unthinkable among young people today – they would think it ludicrous. A virtuoso scholar might, on the other hand, be able to perform quite another feat: he could in a prospectus sketch a few features of a comprehensive system and do it in such a way that it gave the reader (of the prospectus) the impression that he had already read the whole system.

The age of the *encyclopédistes*,[9] the time of those who wrote folios with unremitting application, is past; now it is the turn of those lightly equipped encyclopedists who dispose en passant of the whole of existence and all the sciences. A profound religious renunciation of the world, and of what is of the world,[10] adhered to in daily self-denial, would be unthinkable to the youth of our time; yet every second theology graduate would be virtuoso enough to do something far more marvellous: he would be able to propose a social foundation with no less a goal than to save all who are lost. The age of great and good actions is past; the present age is the age of anticipation. No one is content with doing any definite thing; everyone fondly imagines in reflection that at the least he may discover a new continent. Ours is an age of anticipation; even recognition is accepted in advance. Just as the young man who resolves to get down to serious study for his final exams from 1 September decides to build himself up in the meantime by taking a vacation in the month of August, so the present generation – and this is much harder to understand – seems to have arrived at the serious conclusion that it is the next generation that is to tackle the job in earnest, and in order not to be disturbed or delayed, the present tackles – yes, the banquets. Except that the difference is this: the young man knows he is being irresponsible; the present age is serious – even at the banquets.

There is as little action and decision these days as shallow-water paddlers have a daring desire to swim. But just as the grown-up, tossed about delightedly by the waves, calls to his junior, 'Come on, just jump right in' – so the decision lies, as it were, in existence (but in the individual, naturally) and calls to the younger person not yet exhausted by reflection's excess or overloaded with reflection's fancies, 'Come on, jump in without a care.' Even if it is a reckless leap, so long as it is decisive – if you have it in you to be a man – then the danger and life's stern judgement upon your recklessness will help you become one.

If the jewel that everyone covets lay far out on that very thin crust of ice so that mortal danger watched over it, ensuring that to go out that far would be a perilous venture, while (let's assume this oddity, which is after all only quirky in the imagining) the ice closer to shore was quite safe and frozen to the bottom, then in a passionate age the crowd would cheer their approval of the bold one who risked himself out there. They would tremble for him, and with him, in the peril of his decision, grieve for him in his doom, idolize him should he win the jewel. In a passionless, reflective age it would be an entirely different matter. In mutual appreciation of their shared good sense, they would all sensibly agree that it was certainly not worth going out that far – indeed it would be silly and ridiculous. And then they would transform *enthusiasm's daring* into a *show of artistry* – so as at least to do something, since 'something must be done'. They would go out, on the safe ice, and with the look of connoisseurs judge the expert skaters who could skate just about to the edge (that is, as far as the ice was still safe and not yet into the danger zone) and then swoop to the side. Among the skaters would be one or another who had perfected his art to an exceptional degree. He would be able to perform the trick of making yet another seemingly hazardous swoop right at the very edge, causing the onlookers to cry, 'Ye gods, he's crazy, he is risking his life.' But you see, he is so exceptionally adept that, right enough, he can make a sharp turn at the very edge – that is, where the ice is still quite safe and still short of the danger; just as at the theatre the crowd would shout, 'Bravo!' and greet their performing hero with applause, go home with him in their midst and honour him with a tasty banquet. Good sense would have so much got the upper hand that it would have transformed the task itself into an unreal feat of artistry, and reality into a theatre.

At the banquet in the evening the admiration would reverberate; and while, in the case of true admiration, the admirer is exalted by the thought of being just like the eminent person, humbled by the thought of being unable to have done this great thing himself, ethically encouraged by the ideal of following to the best of his ability this exceptional man's example, here again good sense would have altered the situation. In the glass-clinking admiration at the banquet, even at the moment of elation of the fanfare and the ninefold hurrah, there would be a commonsensical notion that their hero's exploit was not all *that* good, that really it was just a matter of chance that the party was being held for him, since with some practice at tricky turns any one of the participants could have done more or less the same. In short, instead of getting the strength, from this feast of admiration, in discernment and encouragement to do good, the glass-clinkers would rather go home more than ever prone to that most dangerous of all diseases, but also the most fashionable, admiring on the spree, as it were, what one personally considers trivial, because the whole thing has become a theatrical joke – while performing the stimulated clink-clink of admiration in the secret understanding that as near as doesn't matter one might just as well be admiring oneself.

Or if a man did finally put himself at the forefront of an inspired undertaking, and as can easily happen (for eruptive enthusiasm and

judicious apathy are always of a piece) a group of followers joined him
– if now he went to the head of this troop, singing songs of victory
until he approached the moment of decision and danger, and then
turned to speak an inspiring word to the crowd, the whole scene would
change. The *participants* would have judiciously transformed themselves
into a crowd of *spectators*, who now, with the great self-satisfaction of
the judicious, would put on the appearance of being themselves the
ones to have cunningly and ironically tricked him into this enthusiasm,
and of having joined in just to look and laugh at him. And this
exceptional good sense would, in mutual appreciation, satisfy all of
them infinitely, compared to any actual undertaking; to the mind of
the judicious this would be brilliant. Not a word would be heard about
instability, cowardice – no, one would pride oneself on delusion's
scintillating shrewdness, once again making it more difficult for oneself
to be healed. Then the leader too would perhaps lose courage and the
whole thing become as demoralizing as could be, because the excite-
ment turned out to be feigned and an incentive to cowardly conceit.

Standing or falling with one's deeds is no longer the thing; on the
other hand, everybody sits around brilliantly making shift with the help
of some reflection and then with the help of knowing very well what
has to be done. But consider: that which people two by two in
conversation, individually as readers, or as demonstrators in a general
meeting, understand perfectly in the form of reflection and observation,
they would be utterly incapable of understanding in the form of action.
If someone went round and heard what others said ought to be done
and, with a sense of irony, *mir nichts und dir nichts*,[11] then did something
about it, everyone would be aghast; they would find it overhasty.
But then, once they spoke together reflectively about it, they would
understand that indeed it was just what ought to have been done.

The present age which, in its eruptive enthusiasm and then again in
its apathetic indolence, likes so much to poke fun, is itself very close to
being comical. But anyone with a grasp of comedy readily sees that the
comical isn't at all to be found where the present age fancies it is, and
that in our day satire, to be at all beneficial and not cause irreparable
harm, must have as its surety a consistent and well grounded ethical
life-view, a sacrificing disinterestedness, and a high-born nobility that

renounces the moment. Otherwise, the medicine becomes incompar-ably and infinitely more dangerous than the sickness. What is comical is precisely that an age like this even aspires to be witty, and to go in for the comical in such a big way, for this is quite certainly the ultimate and most eye-deceiving evasion. As for the comical, what is there to defy anyway in an age so thoroughly reflected? Lacking passion, it has no emotional collateral in the erotic, no liquid assets of enthusiasm or inwardness in politics and religion, of domesticity, piety or appreciation in daily and social life.

But however stridently the common herd laughs, life scorns the wit that possesses no assets. To aspire to wit without possessing the wealth of inwardness is wanting to be a spendthrift on luxuries yet do without life's necessities; it is, as the proverb says, to sell one's trousers to buy a wig. But a passionless age *has* no assets; everything becomes a transaction in *paper money*. Certain phrases and observations circulate among people, in part true and sensible, yet de-animated; for there is no hero, no lover, no thinker, no knight of faith,[12] no magnanimous person, no one in despair, who vouches for their validity by having experienced them primitively. Just as the rustle of banknotes in our business transactions makes us long to hear the ring of real coins, so we long in the present age for a little primitiveness. But what is more primitive than wit, more primitive even, or at least more surprising, than the first spring bud and the first delicate green stem? Yes, even if spring were to come by arrangement it would still be spring, but a witticism by arrangement would be an abomination. Suppose then that, in succession to the feverishness of eruptive enthusiasm, it came to the point where wit, that divine accidence (and, when it comes, that makeweight to the divine hint from the enigmatic origins of the inexplicable, that makes not even the wittiest man who ever lived dare to say 'Tomorrow' but, worshipfully, 'God willing'),[13] were changed to its shabbiest opposite, a trifling requisite of life, so that it became a profitable trade to manufac-ture and prepare and remake and buy up old and new witticisms – what a dreadful epigram for the witty age!

So, in the end money becomes the object of desire; indeed it too is a promissory note, an abstraction. In the present age even a young man will hardly envy a person his capacities or his skill, or the love of a beautiful girl, or his fame; no, but his money, that is something he will envy. 'Give it me,' the young man will say, 'that will do for me.' And this young man will stray not into reckless actions, he will incur no debt for which repentance is the repayment. He will have nothing to reproach himself for, but he will die under the illusion that had he possessed money he would have lived, maybe even done something great.

Consider the novel. A young man in love, Ferdinand Bergland, is *in love*, but his prudence and reflection thwart him – and the decision he makes is a negative one. Nowadays not even the spontaneity of love is carefree as the lily of the field or in the lovers' eyes more glorious than Solomon in all his splendour.[14] Unconcern bows down under the weight of an erotic criticism and a despondent common sense, and falsifies the value – and the divine glory of the religious cannot come to its assistance – into the highest. A lover abandons his beloved from fear of financial difficulties. How different in the age of revolution when Lusard thoughtlessly, almost without a care, abandons the disgraced girl, leaving all the worries to her; for it is Claudine's merit that she sees the task through, lives on almost nothing, thinks not about her financial difficulties but only of Lusard. But a decision *was* made, and it is this urge to decision that reflection drives away or wants to banish, and the individual suffers the consequences in the form of a dyspeptic, abnormal common sense. Decision in life tries in vain to catch hold of the individual, in vain the benediction awaits the moment of decision; people know well enough how to evade it, prudently and yet taken in, and if this goes on long enough, and they are eventually caught, they are like girls who have been engaged too long, who are seldom well suited to marriage.

After these observations of fact, and in disinterested service to the novel, it would seem appropriate to move from a comparison of the present age with the revolutionary age to a dialectical analysis of the former, and the attendant implications, independently of their presence or absence in the given instant. Incidentally, just as little as in the poetically creative and, if I may so put it, exemplary novel itself, so in this annotative, qua ministering, self-subordinating critique there is no question of which age is the better, or the more significant. The only question is of the 'how' of the age, and this 'how' is gained from a more universal viewpoint, the final consequences of which are arrived at by a conclusion *ab posse ad esse*[15] and verified *ab esse ad posse* by observational experience.

As far as significance goes, it could certainly be that the task of reflection set for the present age will account for itself in a higher existence-form; and as for goodness, the person ensnared in reflection may indeed be just as well intentioned as one who is passionate and resourceful; just as, conversely, there can be as much to say in excuse of the person who goes astray in passion as of the one who on the sly realizes that he is letting himself be deceived by reflection while his fault never becomes public. Another hazard with reflection is not being able to tell whether it is a conclusion reached by deliberation that saves a person from evil deeds, or whether it is exhaustion brought on by the deliberation that saves him, by sapping his strength. But one thing is certain: like all knowledge, reflection too increases sorrow,[16] and above all it is certain that just as for the individual, so too for the whole generation, there is no task or effort harder than to extricate oneself from the temptations of reflection. This is because these temptations are so dialectical, because a single clever invention is able to give the matter a sudden new twist, because reflection is able at any moment to put things in a new light and allow one some measure of escape; for it is possible even in the final moment of reflective decision to do it all over again – after much more exertion than someone with presence of mind needs when in the thick of things. But all this is still, after all, only reflection's excuse, and the position as regards reflection is unchanged because it has been changed only in reflection. Even the fact that the comparison with a previous age does a disservice to the present age, inasmuch as the latter is undergoing the hardship of becoming, is still only a matter of reflection, since the very same circumstance provides it with the uncertainty of hope.

A passionately tumultuous age wants to *overthrow everything, subvert everything*. A revolutionary but passionless and reflecting age changes the manifestation of power into a dialectical sleight-of-hand, *letting everything remain but slyly defrauding it of its meaning; it culminates, instead of in an uprising, in the exhaustion of the inner reality of the relationships, in a reflecting tension that nevertheless lets everything remain; and it has transformed the whole of existence into an equivocation which, in its facticity,[17] is — whereas privately a dialectical fraud surreptitiously substitutes a secret way of reading — that it is not.*

Morality is character; character is something engraved (*charasso*),[18] but the sea has no character, nor does sand, nor abstract common sense, for character is precisely inwardness. Immorality is also character, as energy. Being neither one thing nor the other, on the other hand, is equivocation, and it amounts to equivocation in existence when the qualitative disjunction of qualities is weakened by a gnawing reflection. Passion's uprising is elemental; equivocation's dissolution is a quiet but busy, day-and-night sorites.[19] The distinction between good and evil is enervated by a frivolous, superior, theoretical acquaintance with evil, by an arrogant judiciousness which knows that good is not appreciated and doesn't pay in the world, so almost amounts to stupidity. No one is carried away by good into great exploits, no one is precipitated by evil into glaring sin; the one is just as good as the other; and yet for that very reason there is all the more to talk about, for equivocation is an exciting stimulant and quite otherwise verbose than is joy over the good or than is aversion to evil.

The coiled springs of life relationships, which exist only by virtue of the qualitatively distinguishing passion, lose their resilience; the qualitative expression of the distance between those who differ from each other is no longer the law for a relation in inwardness to each other, in the relationship. Inwardness is lacking, and the relationship to that extent doesn't exist, or it is a supine cohesion. For the negative law is to be unable to do without each other, yet unable to stay together; the positive law is to be able to do without each other, yet to be able to stay together; or, still positively, to be unable to do without each other because of the cohesion. Instead of inwardness there enters another relation: the distinct does not relate to its distinctness, but it's as if the pair stand there and keep an eye on each other, and *this tension is really the ending of the relationship*. This is not that cheerful, outspoken admiration which, quick to express appreciation, now doffs its hat to distinction, is now shocked by its pride and arrogance; nor is it the opposite relation, not at all – admiration and distinction become pretty well a pair of courteous equals keeping an eye on each other. This is not the burgher who with cheerful loyalty pays homage to the king and now is embittered by his tyranny; far from it – being a burgher becomes something else, it means being a *third party*. The burgher does not relate himself in the relationship, he is a spectator working out this problem: the relationship between a king and his subject; because time goes by in the appointment of committee upon committee – as long at least as there are still a number who want with total passion and each for himself to be this definite thing he is supposed to be. But finally it will end with the whole age becoming a committee. This is not the father who in indignation brings his fatherly authority to bear in a single curse, nor the son who defies him, a falling-out which may still end in the inwardness of reconciliation. No, the relationship in itself is irreproachable, for it is more likely to come to an end in any case, in so far as the parties do not relate essentially to each other in the relationship, the relationship itself being now a problem in which, as in a card game, the parties keep a watch on each other instead of relating to each other, count the expressions of the relationship ('in each other's mouth'),[20] instead of the resolute devotion of the relationship; because a long time passes as more and more have to renounce the modest yet so copious and God-pleasing tasks of the quieter life in order to realize something higher, in order to think over the relationships in a higher relation.

But, in the end, the whole generation becomes a representation – representing . . . well, there's no saying who; a representation that thinks over the relations . . . well, it's hard to say for whose sake. This is not the difficult adolescent who nevertheless quakes and trembles before his schoolmaster. No, the relation is sooner one of a certain impartiality in a mutual exchange between teacher and pupil on how to run a good school. Going to school does not mean quaking and trembling, nor does it mean just learning, but practically also interesting oneself in the problem of school education. The distinction between man and woman is not breached here in blatant dissipation, no, never – propriety is observed in such a way that it may always be said of the particular borderline case of 'innocent' philandering that it is a trifle.

What should one call such a relation? I think 'tension', but not, be it noted, a tension that strains every nerve for a decisive turn of events, but a tension rather in which existence is exhausted – the ardour, enthusiasm and inwardness lost that make the chains of dependency and the crown of dominion light, that make the child's obedience and the father's authority happy, that make the humility of admiration and the eminence of distinction light-hearted, that give the teacher a uniquely valid meaning and thus the pupil the opportunity to learn, that unite the woman's frailty and the man's power in the equal strength of devotion. The relation is still there, but without the resilience to concentrate itself in inwardness so as to bring about a harmonious union. The relations announce their presence, yet as absent; not in a full-bodied way but more in a sort of shuffling, half-asleep incessancy.

Let me give quite a simple illustration to show what I mean. I was once a visitor in a family that had a clock whose mechanism was in some way out of order. But the trouble did not show in the spring suddenly whirring, the chain breaking, or even in a failure to strike; on the contrary, it went on striking but in a curious, abstractly normal but nevertheless confusing way. It did not strike twelve at twelve o'clock and then one at one o'clock, but at regular intervals struck just once. All day it went on striking in this way, yet never giving the hour. Likewise with a debilitating tension: the circumstances remain but in a state of abstract incessancy that prevents any breakdown; things appear that may be called manifestations of the circumstances, yet in their appearance they are not only imprecise but almost meaningless. The calming factor is that things stay the way they are, their facticity; what is dangerous is that this is just what encourages reflection's subtle gnawing away. Against rebellion one can use force, and punishment awaits the demonstrably false witness, but it is hard to get rid of dialectical secretiveness; it already takes quite a sharp ear to trace the soundless tread of reflection as it steals down the secret path of equivocation.

The established order stands, but passionless reflection is calmed by the fact that it is an equivocation. One doesn't want to abolish the monarchy, no, never; but if one could have it little by little transformed into illusion, one would gladly shout, 'Hurrah for the King!' One doesn't want to have eminence brought down, no, never; but at the same time, if one could spread the knowledge that it is an illusion – then one would admire it. One can let the entire Christian terminology stand, but in the private knowledge that it is not supposed to mean anything decisive. And there will be no call to repent since, after all, one isn't tearing anything down. One would no more want a powerful monarch than an energetic champion of freedom, or a religious plenipotentiary. No, one quite innocently wants to let the established order stand – but while being increasingly aware, in a reflective knowledge, that it *isn't* standing. And one would be proud to imagine this was irony, as though in an era of negativity the true ironist weren't the hidden enthusiast (just as the hero is the manifest enthusiast in a positive era), as though the true ironist were not self-sacrificial, seeing that the grand master himself, after all, ended by being punished by death.[21]

In the end, the tension of reflection assumes the status of a principle and, just as in a passionate age *enthusiasm* is *the unifying principle*, so *envy* becomes *the negatively unifying principle* in a passionless and very reflective age. Yet one mustn't straight away take this ethically as an accusation; no, reflection's idea, if one may put it this way, is envy, and the envy is therefore twofold: a selfish envy in the individual, and then again the envy that the surroundings direct towards him. Reflection's envy in the individual frustrates impassioned decision in him, and if it looks as if he were just about to succeed, the reflected opposition of the surroundings stops him. Reflection's envy holds will and energy as though in captivity. The individual must then first of all break out of the prison in which his own reflection holds him, and if he then succeeds he still does not stand in the open but in the vast penitentiary formed by the reflection of the surroundings; and he is related to this again through the reflection-relation in himself, from which only religious inwardness can free him, however much he sees through the falseness of that relation. But that it is a prison that reflection holds both the individual and the age in, that it is reflection that does it and not tyrants or secret police, nor priests or aristocrats – is a view of things that reflection does all in its power to prevent, maintaining the flattering illusion that the possibilities offered by reflection are something far greater than paltry decision. The selfish form of envy, in the form of desire, demands too much of the individual himself and impedes him by spoiling him, like a weak mother's partiality; for envy in himself prevents the individual from becoming devoted. Envy in the surroundings, in which the individual himself again relates to others, is of a negatively critical kind.

But the longer this continues, the more reflection's envy will acquire the status of ethical envy. Confined air always becomes noxious, and similarly, confinement in reflection, with no action or event to provide ventilation, develops that censorious envy. While in the tension of reflection the better energies keep each other in check, baseness rises to the surface, its impudence impressing like a kind of force and its contemptuousness becoming its protective privilege, because it allows it to escape envy's attention.

Besides, it is deeply embedded in human nature not to be able to stay on top without a break and keep on admiring; it calls for change. Which is why even the most enthusiastic age requires an envious joke at the expense of excellence. This is perfectly in order and may be quite appropriate if someone, after the Shrovetide merrymaking with the excellent, turning his gaze once more upon it, is able to find it unchanged. For otherwise he will have lost more by joking than the joke was worth. There can be scope for envy in this way even in an enthusiastic age; and yes, envy, even if the age is less enthusiastic, so long as it still has the energy to endow envy with character and is clear in its mind what expressing it means, envy can have its own, albeit perilous, significance. Thus in Greece, for example, ostracism was an expression of envy, a kind of balance-restoring self-defence against excellence. It was practised in full consciousness of its dialectical implication, namely that ostracism was a mark of excellence. In representing a rather earlier era in Greece it would therefore be ironic in the spirit of Aristophanes to have an utterly insignificant man sent into exile by ostracism. This irony would constitute even higher comedy than ironically, say, letting a nobody like that become ruler, simply because exile by ostracism is already the negative expression of excellence. This is why it would in turn be a still higher ironical comedy to have it all end with the people recalling the banished one because they couldn't get on without him – which would have to be a total enigma to those he lived in exile with, since naturally they would have been unable to find any excellence in him at all. In *The Knights*, Aristophanes portrays the ultimate state of decay when, just as the Dalai Lama's excrement is revered, the rabble ends by adoring, or adoringly contemplating, its reflection in the first and best of the trash — a situation that, in its degeneracy, corresponds in terms of popular government to putting imperial dignity up for auction.

But if envy still has character, ostracism is a negative honour. The man who told Aristides that he voted to banish him 'because he couldn't bear hearing him called the only just man' did not deny Aristides' excellence but was admitting something about himself: that his relation to this excellence was not that of the happy infatuation of admiration, but that of the unhappy infatuation of envy. But he did not disparage that excellence.

On the other hand, the more reflection gains the upper hand in developing lethargy, the more dangerous becomes the envy, because it then lacks the character to be aware of its own meaning; but responding to events in a characterless, evasively vacillating and cowardly manner, envy re-explains the same utterance in all sorts of ways — it wants it to be a joke, and if it sees that this doesn't work it then says it was meant as an insult, and if that doesn't work, then it wasn't anything at all; it wants it to be a witticism, and if that doesn't produce a response it explains that it wasn't meant in that way either, it was ethical satire, something people should be concerned with; and if this miscarries, then it says it was nothing and no one's concern. Envy assumes the status of the principle of lack of character, which wants to sneak up out of baseness to make itself into something, constantly protecting itself by conceding that it is nothing. Envy, lacking character, does not understand that excellence is excellence, does not see that it is itself a negative acknowledgement of excellence but wants to bring it down, have excellence disparaged until it is in fact no longer excellence. And envy directs itself against the excellence that is, as well as against that which is to come.

This self-*establishing* envy is *levelling*, and while a passionate age *accelerates, raises and topples, extols and oppresses*, a reflective, passionless age does the opposite — *it stifles and impedes, it levels*. Levelling is a quiet, mathematically abstract affair that avoids all fuss. While the eruptive short-term enthusiasm might look despondently for some misfortune, just to taste the strength of existence, no interruption can help the apathy that succeeds it, any more than it helps the levelling engineer. If an uprising at its peak is like a volcanic explosion in which not a word can be heard, then levelling at its peak is like a deathly stillness over which nothing can raise itself but into which everything impotently sinks down.

At the head of an uprising may be a single man, but no single man can take the lead in levelling, for then he would be the master and would have escaped the levelling. The single individual may assist in levelling, each in his own little group, but levelling is an abstract power and is abstraction's victory over the individuals. In modern times levelling is reflection's equivalent to fate in antiquity. The dialectic of antiquity pointed to prominence (the single great one – and then the crowd; one free and then the slaves); the dialectic of Christianity points for the time being to representation (the majority views itself in the representative; is liberated by the awareness, in a kind of self-consciousness, that it is they whom he is representing). The dialectic of the present age points to impartiality, and its most consistent if mistaken implementation is levelling, as the negative unity of the negative mutuality of the individuals.

Anyone may readily see that levelling has its deep significance in the ascendancy of the category of the generation over that of individuality. Whereas in antiquity the mass of individuals existed, as it were, to fix the price of the excellent individual, today the monetary standard has changed so that *in equal proportions* about so-and-so many human beings make one individual, so that it's just a matter of getting the right number – then one has significance. In antiquity the individual in the crowd meant nothing at all – the man of excellence meant all of them. The present age points in the direction of mathematical proportionality, so that, in roughly proportional measure in all estates, so-and-so many make one individual. The eminent personage dared to allow himself everything, the individuals in the crowd nothing at all. Nowadays one understands that so-and-so many make one individual, and one quite logically counts oneself together with a few others (true, we call it uniting, but that is being polite) in the most trivial thing. For no other reason than to realize a whim one counts oneself together with a few and one does it – that is, one dares to do it. This is why in the end not even a very gifted person is able to liberate himself from reflection, for in the most trivial thing he soon realizes that he is only a fraction and loses the chance of religiousness's infinite liberation.

Even if an association of several people had the courage to meet death, that today would not mean to say that each individual had the courage to do so. For what the individual feared more than death would be reflection's judgement upon him, reflection's objection to his wanting to venture something as an individual. The individual does not belong to God, nor to himself, nor to his beloved, nor to his art, nor to his scholarship; no, just as a serf belongs to an estate, so the individual realizes that in every respect he belongs to an abstraction under which reflection subsumes him. If, in our time, a group of people, each one individually, were able to decide to give all their fortune to some good cause or other, it would not follow that the individual himself could do the same; and again, not because he was in two minds about renouncing his fortune, but because much more than poverty he feared the judgement of reflection. If ten people could agree to vouch for love's full and unqualified validity or – and without any crippling reflection – for the unlimited justification of enthusiasm, it would not follow that each of the ten could do so individually; for, even more than the bliss of love and bearing witness with their spirit,[22] they would ambiguously love the judgement of reflection – so ten would have to be doing something that it is contradictory for more than one to do. The idolized positive principle of sociality in our time is the consuming, demoralizing principle, which in the thraldom of reflection transforms even virtues into *vitia splendida*.[23] And to what can this be due other than to a disregard for the singling out of the religious individual before God in the responsibility of eternity? When terror begins here, one seeks comfort in company, and reflection then captures the individual for life. And those who didn't even notice this crisis beginning fall without further ado under the relation of reflection.

Levelling is not a single individual's action but an activity of reflection in the hands of an abstract power. Just as one calculates the diagonal in a parallelogram of forces,[24] so too can one calculate the law of levelling. For the individual who himself levels a few is carried along too, and so it goes on. Therefore, while the individual egoistically thinks he knows what he is doing, of all of them one has to say that they know *not* what they do,[25] for just as a something more that is not just the individuals' emerges in the unanimity of enthusiasm, so too here a something more emerges. One conjures up a demon to which no individual is equal, and while in the brief moment of levelling's pleasure the individual selfishly enjoys the abstraction, he is also putting his signature to his own downfall. The forward thrust of the enthusiast *may* end with his downfall, but the success of the leveller is *eo ipso* his downfall. The scepticism of levelling is something no age can halt, no age itself, nor the present age, for the very moment it wants to halt levelling it will merely confirm the law once again. Halting it is possible only if, individually singled out, the individual achieves the fearlessness of religiousness. I once saw a fight in which three men shamefully mis-treated a fourth. The crowd stood and watched with indignation; its own murmurs of disapproval began to spur it to action. One or two in the crowd got together, took hold of one of the assailants and threw him to the ground, etc. That is to say, the avengers were confirming the same law as the assailants. If I can be allowed to bring my own humble person into the picture I can complete the story. I went up to one of the avengers and attempted to explain dialectically the inconsist-ency of their behaviour, but it was evidently quite impossible for him to enter into any exchange of the sort. All he did was repeat: 'It serves him right: a scoundrel like that deserves to be three to one.' There's comedy here, to be sure, especially for someone who didn't see how it began but heard one man say of another that he (the lone man) was three to one just when the opposite was the case: there were three against him. One thing would be the comedy of contradiction, as in when the watchman asked the solitary person to disperse, and the other is the comedy of the self-contradiction itself. But what seemed clear to me was that the better course was to abandon any hope of ending this scepticism, lest it be continued against me.

No single man – the eminent person in terms of superiority and of the dialectic of fate – will be able to halt levelling's abstraction, for the single man's is a negative elevation and the age of heroes is over. No congregation will be in a position to halt levelling's abstraction, because in the context of reflection the congregation is itself in the service of levelling. Not even the individualities of nations will be able to halt it, for the abstraction of levelling reflects on a higher negativity, namely that of pure humanity. The abstraction of levelling, this spontaneous combustion of the human race produced by the friction arising when the individual, singling out inwardly in religiousness, fails to materialize, will be 'constant', as they say of a trade-wind; this abstraction consumes everything, but by means of it every individual, each for himself, may again be educated religiously, helped in the highest sense in the *examen rigorosum*[26] of levelling to gain the essentiality of the religious in himself. For the younger person who from the start realizes, however firmly he himself clings to what to him is admirable, that levelling is what the selfish individual and the selfish generation took for evil[27] but also something for the individual, each for himself, if honestly to God he wills it, can be the point of departure for the highest life – for him it will be genuinely educative to live in an age of levelling. Contemporaneity will, in the highest sense, have for him the ability to be religiously formative, and to be educational both aesthetically and intellectually, inasmuch as the comic will absolutely make its presence felt. For the height of comedy is precisely the subsuming of the single individual, with no middle term, under the infinitely abstract idea of pure humanity, inasmuch as all the organizational ways of concretizing individuality that temper the comical with relativity and provide the strength of a relative pathos, are consumed. But this again expresses the fact that salvation comes only through the essentiality of the religious in the single individual. And it will be an inspiration for him to realize that precisely this going astray gives the individual access to the highest, each for himself, if he is magnanimous enough to want it. But the levelling must go on, it has to happen, just as offence must needs come into the world, but woe unto him by whom it comes.[28]

It is often said that a reformation has to begin with each person reforming himself. That, however, has not happened, because the idea of reformation has given birth to a hero, one who as such surely bought his appointment from God quite dearly. By attaching themselves to him directly, individuals acquire that costly purchase for a better, indeed a bargain, price, but they do not acquire the highest. The abstraction of levelling, on the other hand, is a principle that like the keen easterly wind enters into no intimate relation with the single individual but only into the relation of abstraction, which is the same for all. So no hero suffers for others or helps others; levelling itself becomes the strict taskmaster that looks after the rearing. And the person who learns the most from the rearing, and becomes the greatest, does not become the man of distinction, the hero, the one who stands out – this is prevented by levelling, which is consistent to the very end; and this person prevents it himself because he has grasped the meaning of levelling – no, he only becomes an essential human being in the full-bodied sense of equality. This is religiousness's Idea. But the rearing is rigorous and the returns seemingly very meagre – seemingly, for if the individual is unwilling to learn to be satisfied with himself in the essentiality of religiousness, before God rather than ruling over the world; unwilling to be satisfied with ruling over himself, as a priest, with being his own audience, as an author, with being his own reader, etc.; if he is unwilling to learn to be inspired by this as the noblest he should achieve because it expresses equality before God and equality with all men, then he will not escape reflection; and then he may experience in respect of his talent one moment of delusion when he believes it is he who is doing the levelling, until he succumbs to the levelling himself.

It doesn't help to appeal to or to summon a Holger Danske[29] or a Martin Luther. Their age is past, and it is really self-indulgence on the part of individuals to want something of that sort, the impatience of finitude that wants to have cheaply and at second hand what is bought dearly at first hand. It doesn't help to found society upon society, for negatively something higher has been posited, even though the short-sighted society man cannot see it. In its immediate and beautiful formation, the individuality principle in the guise of the man of excellence, the man of rank, is a preliminary form of the generation, and it has the subordinate individuals form themselves in groups around the representative. In its eternal truth, this principle uses the abstraction and impartiality of the generation in levelling and in that way religiously develops the individual, with his concurrence, into an essential human being. For, impotent as levelling is with respect to the eternal, with respect to anything temporary it is overpowering. Reflection is a sling one is strapped into, but through the inspired leap of religiousness things change, and it becomes a sling that throws one into the embrace of the eternal. And reflection is, and remains, the most unyielding creditor in life. It has up until now astutely bought up all possible life-views, but the eternal life-view of essential religiousness is one that it cannot buy. On the other hand, it can tempt people away from anything else with wonderful illusions, and discourage them from anything else by reminding them of the past. But by leaping out into the depths one learns to help oneself, love all others as much as oneself, however much one is accused of arrogance and pride, for not accepting help – or of selfishness, for not wanting slyly to deceive others by helping them, by helping them to miss their chance of achieving what is highest of all.

If anyone says that what I propose here is common knowledge and something anyone can say, my answer is: So much the better, I seek no prominence, I have nothing against everyone knowing it, unless the fact that everyone knows and can say it means it is taken from me and lodged in the negative commonality. As long as I am allowed to keep hold of it, it loses none of its value for me by everyone knowing it.

The modern age has in reality tended towards levelling through many upheavals, none of which *was* levelling, however, since none of them was abstract enough but was still part of concrete reality. There can be an approximate levelling through one prominence bearing down on another, so that both are weakened; there can be approximate levelling through one prominence being neutralized by another, through an association of the individually weaker becoming stronger than the single prominence; there can be approximate levelling by a single estate, e.g. the clergy, the burghers, the peasantry, the people themselves; but all this is still only abstraction working within concrete relations of individuals.

For levelling really to come about a phantom must first be provided, its spirit, a monstrous abstraction, an all-encompassing something that is nothing, a mirage – this phantom is *the public*. Only a passionless but reflective age can spin this phantom out, with the help of the press when the press itself becomes an abstraction. In spirited times, times of passionate upheaval, even when a people wants to put the desolate idea of destruction and total subversion into effect, at least there is no public; there are parties and there is concreteness. The press will in such times itself assume the concrete character of the disarray. But just as sedentary professionals are especially prone to spin fantasies, so too a passionless, sedentary, reflective age, when the press, itself weak, is supposed to be the only thing that can keep life going in the prevailing torpor, will spin out this phantom. The public is levelling's real master, for when levelling is only approximate there is something it levels with, while the public is a monstrous nothing.

The public is a concept that cannot possibly occur in antiquity. A people itself had to appear en masse, *in corpore*, at the scene of the action, had to take responsibility for what the single individual from its midst did, while the single individual in turn had to be there personally and, as this particular individual, had to submit to the summary court's approval or disapproval. It is only when no energetic association gives substance to the concretion that the press creates this abstraction, the public, composed as it is of unreal individuals who are not and never can be united in the contemporaneousness of a situation or organization, and who nevertheless, it is insisted, are a whole. The public is a corps, more numerous than all the people together; but this corps can never be marshalled for inspection – indeed, it cannot have even so much as a single representative because it is itself an abstraction. And yet, if the age is passionless, reflective, erasing all that is concrete, the public becomes the whole that is supposed to include everything. But this situation again means precisely that the single individual is assigned to himself.

In the contemporaneity of the real moment and the real situation with real people, each of whom is something, there is support for the single individual. But the existence of the public makes for no situation and no assembly. The single individual who reads is, after all, not a public, and if little by little many individuals read – and perhaps everyone does – there is still no contemporaneity. The public may take a year and a day to 'assemble', and once it has done so it still does not exist. As you would expect, the abstraction formed paralogistically by individuals, instead of helping them, makes them recoil from one another. Someone who, with actual persons in the contemporaneity of the actual moment and situation, has no opinion of his own adopts the majority's opinion, or, if more inclined to be combative, the minority's. But note that the majority and the minority are actual human beings, and this is why resorting to them is supportive. The public, however, is an abstraction. To adopt the same opinion as these or those particular persons is to know that they would be subject to the same danger as oneself, that they would err with one if the opinion were wrong, etc. But to adopt the same opinion as the public is a treacherous consolation, for the public exists only *in abstracto*. So, while there has never been a majority so positively certain of being in the right and having the upper hand as the public, this is but little consolation for the single individual, for the public is a phantom that allows no personal approach. If someone adopts the public opinion today, and tomorrow is booed, it is the public that boos. A generation, a people, a general assembly, a community, a man – all still have a responsibility through being something, can be ashamed of being inconstant and disloyal; but a public remains the public. A people, an assembly, a human being can change in a way that allows one to say they are no longer the same; but the public can become the very opposite and is still the same – the public. The individual, however, by this very abstraction and abstract disciplining (in so far as he is not already formed in his own inwardness), will, if not destroyed in the process, be in the highest religious sense educated to be satisfied with himself and with his relationship to God, to make up his own mind instead of agreeing with the public, which eats up all the relative and concrete in individuality; and instead of keeping on counting heads will find his point of rest in himself before God. And this will be the absolute difference between the modern era and antiquity, namely that the totality is not the concretion that supports, that educates the individual though without developing him absolutely; but an abstraction which, in its abstract indifference, by repelling him helps him to become wholly educated – unless he is destroyed. What was discouraging about antiquity was that the man of distinction was what others *could not be*; the inspiring thing will be that the person who gains himself religiously is no more than what *all can be*.

The public is not a people, a generation, one's era, nor a religious community, a society, nor such and such particular people, for all these are what they are only by virtue of what is concrete. No, not a single one of those who belong to the public has an essential engagement in anything. You might say that a person belongs to the public for a few hours a day, that is, during the hours when he is nothing; because during the hours in which he is the definite person he is, he does not belong to the public. Composed of units like that, of individuals in the moments when they are nothing, the public is a kind of monstrous something or other, that abstract waste and emptiness that is all and nothing. But, for the same reason, anyone can commandeer a public, a public is something anyone can pick up, even a drunken sailor pre-senting a peep-show,[30] just as the Roman Catholic Church speciously expanded itself by appointing bishops *in partibus infidelium*;[31] and the drunken sailor has in terms of dialectical consistency absolutely the same right to a public as the most distinguished, the absolute right to place all these many, many zeros before his number one. The public is all and nothing, it is the most dangerous of all powers and the most meaningless: one may speak to a whole nation in the name of the public, yet the public is less than even a single quite unremarkable actual human being. The category of the public is that phantom of reflection whose trickery has made individuals vain, since this monster, compared to which the concretions of reality appear trifling, is something anyone can pretend to. The public is the age of common sense's own fairy-tale, in imagination* it makes individuals greater than kings over a people; but then again, the public is the cruel abstraction by which individuals will be religiously educated – or destroyed.

The abstraction of the press (for a newspaper, a journal, is no political concretion and only in an abstract sense an individual), combined with the passionlessness and reflectiveness of the age, gives birth to that abstraction's phantom, the public, which is the real leveller. This too, apart from its negative implications for the religious life, can have its significance. But the less idea there is in an age, and the more it relaxes

---

* Luckily, as an author I have never sought or had any public, but have been well content with 'that individual' [the dedicatee of Kierkegaard's numerous 'edifying discourses' – trans.], for which restriction I have become almost proverbial.

in indolent recovery from the exhaustion of eruptive enthusiasm – if we also imagined the press becoming weaker and weaker because no big event or idea gripped the age – the more readily levelling becomes a decadent urge, a sensory stimulant that tickles for a moment and only makes bad worse, the conditions of salvation harder, and the probability of destruction greater. And if people have often portrayed the demoralization of autocracy and the decadence of revolutionary periods, the decadence of a passionless age is just as corrupt, even if its ambiguity makes it less striking. It can be of interest and importance, therefore, to give it a thought. In a state of enervated lethargy more and more individuals will aspire to be nothing – in order to be the public, this abstract whole formed, laughably, by the participant becoming a third party. This inert crowd that understands nothing itself and has nothing it wants to do, this gallery-public, tries now to pass the time, indulging in the fancy that all that anyone does happens just so as to give it something to chat about. Inertness sits there, aloof, legs crossed, and everyone willing to work – the king, the public official, the teacher of the people, the more capable journalist, the poet, the artist – will be hitched up to drag that inertness along, which aloofly believes the others to be the horses.

Were I to imagine this public as a person (for although some of the better ones belong momentarily to the public, they still possess an organizing concretion that keeps them firm, even if they fail to gain religiousness's most high), most likely I would think of one or other Roman emperor, a large, well fed figure who suffers from boredom and therefore craves only the sensory stimulation of laughter, for the divine gift of wit is not worldly enough. So to relieve the monotony this person saunters about, more inert than evil, but negatively power-hungry. Anyone who has read the ancient authors knows the number of things an emperor could think up to make time pass more quickly. The public in the same way keeps a dog for its amusement. This dog is literary contempt. If someone superior appears, even someone of distinction, the dog is prodded and the fun begins. The snapping dog tears at his coat-tails, indulges in all sorts of unmannerly rudeness – until the public tires of it and says, 'That will do now.' The public has then levelled. The better one, the stronger one, has been maltreated – and the dog, well, yes, it is still a dog, which the public itself holds in contempt. Thus the levelling occurs through a third party; nothingness's public has levelled through a third party which, in its contemptibleness, was already more than levelled and less than nothing. And the public is unrepentant, for it was not the public, it was the dog – just as one tells children the cat did it. And the public is unrepentant because what it did was not really demeaning – just a bit of fun. Now, had the instrument of levelling been some remarkable capacity, the indolent public would have been fooled, for then that instrument would have been yet another interference to be levelled. But when superiority is kept down by contemptibleness, and contemptibleness kept down by itself, then this is nothingness's riddance. And the public will be unrepentant, for it is not really they who have the dog, they only subscribe; nor did they incite the dog directly to attack, nor was it straightforwardly they that whistled it off. In the event of a lawsuit the public would say, 'The dog is not mine, it has no owner.' And if the dog were picked up and sent off to the veterinary school to be put down, the public would still be able to say that, really, it was a good thing the bad dog was put down; that's what we all wanted – even the subscribers.

Perhaps someone putting himself reflectively into a situation of this kind is inclined to focus on the superior one who suffered the maltreatment, and thinks a grave misfortune befell him. I cannot at all agree, for such experience does the person good who wants to be helped towards the most high, and it is something he rather should wish for, even if others may be upset on his account. No, what is awful is something else – the thought of the many human lives that are forfeited, or easily may be. I won't even mention the lost or the led astray unto perdition, those who for money play the role of the dog, but the many unsettled ones, the irresponsible, the sensual, those who in their superior vapidity acquire no deeper impression of life than this foolish simpering; all the poor souls who are led into new temptation because in their small-mindedness they even derive self-importance from having sympathy for the assaulted, without grasping that it is always the assaulted who are the strongest in such a situation, without grasping that here, though with an awful yet ironic emphasis, it is a matter of: Weep not for him, but weep for yourselves.[32]

This situation is the lowest kind of levelling, because levelling always corresponds to the common factor in terms of which all are made equal. Thus eternal life is also a kind of levelling, and yet it is not so; for the common factor is in the religious sense to be an essentially human being.

From these dialectical categories and their implications, independent of the actual presence or absence of the latter in the given instance, from the dialectical view of the present age itself, I now proceed to a dialectical grasp of the more concrete attributes in terms of which the present age appears in the novelistic version's reflecting of them in domestic and social life. Here it is the shadowy side that becomes apparent, and even if there is no denying its facticity, it is nevertheless also certain that just as reflection itself is not the evil, so too may a very reflective age also have its bright side, precisely because a good deal of reflectiveness is the precondition of a meaningfulness that is greater than immediate passion – is the precondition of it if enthusiasm steps in and guides the powers of reflection into decision; and because a good deal of reflectiveness raises the average level of efficiency in the prerequisites for action – if religiousness steps in and takes over those prerequisites in the individual. Reflection is not the evil, but the reflective condition and stagnation in reflection are the abuse and the corruption that, by transforming the prerequisites into evasions, bring about regression.

The present age is essentially a sensible age, dispassionate, for which reason it has *annulled the principle of contradiction*. From this consideration we can deduce the variety of features that the author with his fine artistry and elevated composure has so disinterestedly rendered. For, naturally, the author's own opinion is nowhere discernible, he merely reproduces the reflected image. One can say in general of a passionless but reflective age, compared to a passionate one, that *it gains in extensity what is loses in intensity*. But this extensity may become in turn the condition for a higher form, if a corresponding intensity takes over what is extensively at its disposal.

In existence, nullifying the principle of contradiction is the expression for being in contradiction with oneself. The creative omnipotence implicit in the passion of the absolute disjunction that brings the individual into the closure of agreement with himself is transformed into the extensity of common sense and reflection: through knowing and being everything possible, being in contradiction with oneself – that is, being just nothing. The principle of contradiction strengthens the individual in faithfulness to himself, so that, just as that resolute number three that Socrates speaks of so beautifully would rather endure anything than become the number four[33] or even a very large round number, he would rather be small but faithful to himself than all sorts of things in contradiction with himself.

What is it to *chat*? It is to have repealed the passionate disjunction between being silent and speaking. Only the person who can remain essentially silent can essentially speak; only the person who can remain essentially silent can essentially act. Silence is inwardness. Talking forestalls essential speaking, and reflection's utterance weakens action by stealing a march on it. But the person who can speak essentially because he can keep silent will not have a whole world to speak of – just the one thing – and he will find time both to speak and stay silent.[34] Talkativeness gains in extensity: it has everything to talk about and goes on incessantly. In an age when individuals are not turned inwards in religious inwardness, quietly content, comfortably satisfied, but in the relationship of reflection search outwardly and for each other, when no great event ties the loose ends together in the unanimity of great change – the talking begins. The great event gives the passionate age (for the two go together) something to speak about; all want to speak about the same one thing – the poets sing about nothing else, it is alone what conversations echo, the greetings of passers-by contain references to this one thing. It is one and the same. Chatting, on the other hand, has a great deal to chat about. And so, when the important event was over, when silence returned, there was at least something to remember, something to think about, while one was silent; whereas a new generation speaks of quite different things. But chat dreads the moment of silence that would make the emptiness plain.

What proves to be the law regarding poetic production is the same, on a smaller scale, as that for every person's life in social interchange and education. Anyone who experiences something originally also experiences, through ideality,[35] the possibilities of the same and the possibility of the opposite. These possibilities are his literary legal property. But his own private, personal actuality is not. His speaking, his producing, are thus borne by silence. The ideal perfection of his speaking, his producing, will correspond to his silence, and the absolute expression of that silence will be that the ideality contains the qualitatively opposite possibility. As soon as the productive artist gives up his own actuality, its facticity, he is no longer essentially productive; his beginning will be his end, and the first word already a sin against the holy modesty of ideality. A poetic presentation of this kind is therefore also, from an aesthetic point of view, a kind of private talkativeness and easily recognizable by the absence in equal measure of its opposite. For ideality is to deal fairly with the opposite. The person who is creative out of unhappiness, for example, will, if genuinely initiated into ideality, have as great a preference for writing about happiness as about unhappiness. But the silence with which he brackets off his own personal actuality is precisely the condition of his gaining ideality; otherwise, despite all precautions, such as setting the scene in Africa, etc., he will be recognizable by his one-sided preference. For an author must certainly, like everyone else, have his private personality, but this must be his *aduton*,[36] and just as one bars the entrance to a house by stationing there two soldiers with crossed bayonets, so the dialectical cross of qualitative opposites forms the equal dealing of ideality that prevents all access.

But what is true here of the larger context, where it is most clearly evident (which is why it was mentioned), is true also on a lesser scale in the smaller context. Here again, silence is the condition, in man's conversation with man, of cultivated interchange. The more ideality and idea a person silently possesses, the more able he will be even in his daily intercourse to regenerate everyday life and the lives of everyday people in a way that makes it sound as if he speaks only from a distance, even about this or that particular fact. The less ideality and the more extroversion, the more the conversation will tend towards trivial patter and the dropping of names, 'absolutely reliable' private intelligence on what this and that named person has said, etc.; a chattering of confidences about what one oneself wants and does not want, now plans to achieve, would have said on that occasion, about what girl one is courting, why one nevertheless doesn't want to get married, etc. In human intercourse the inwardness of silence is the condition of cultivated speech; to chat is inwardness's twisting, inside-out extroversion, lack of cultivation.

In the novel one finds excellent examples of this kind of chatting, a matter of mere trifles but always about specific persons mentioned by name, whose trivial circumstances are interesting as much as anything for their names. Just as the precentor, Link,[37] thinks he has spoken with Sophie although all she said was 'No', so there are many long conversations in which it seems something was said, a great deal indeed, just because names are mentioned. A person who chats must presumably chat about something, since the aim is to have something to chat about; but this something is not something in the sense of ideality, for in that case one speaks. It is something only in the sense of being a trivial fact: that Mr Madsen has become engaged and given his sweetheart a Persian shawl, that Petersen the poet plans to write a new book of verse, that Marcussen the actor mispronounced a word last night.

Suppose a law could be enforced – we can imagine it – suppose, that is, a law was made that didn't forbid people to speak but merely enjoined that everything spoken about had to be spoken about as though it happened fifty years ago. All the chatterers would be done for, they would despair, and yet it couldn't interfere with those genuinely able to speak. An actor's mispronunciation of a word can be of real interest only if there is something remarkable in the slip of the tongue itself, and in that case the fifty years would make no difference – but Miss Gusta, for example, would be miserable; she who had been to the theatre herself that very evening, had sat in the box with the commercial counsellor's lady, Mrs Waller, who had herself detected the mispronunciation and even seen one of the chorus laughing about it, etc. But it would indeed be a pity and a cruel fate for all these talkative people who, after all, also have to live; but that of course is why the law is just a *posito*.[38]

Because of this chatting the distinction between private and public is nullified in a private–public chattiness, which is just about what the public amounts to. For the public is that publicity that is interested in what is for the most part private. What no one would dare present to a meeting, what no one would be able to *speak* about, what even chatterers would scarcely admit to having chatted about, can very well be put in writing for the public and known by them in the guise of the public.

What is *formlessness*? It is the repealed passionate distinction between form and content, which therefore, in contrast to insanity and stupidity, may contain truth, but the truth it contains can never be essentially true. Formlessness will be able to expand in extensity, comprehensively, attacking on all fronts, in contrast to essential content which has the inadequate limitation of its firmness, if you will, intensively present in self-deepening. The ubiquity of formlessness in a passionless, reflective age finds expression, besides in the frivolous dallying between the most diverse people, in its opposite: a ruling penchant and desire to act 'for the sake of principle'. *Principium*, as the word indicates, is what is primary, that is, the substantial, the idea in the unopened form of feeling and enthusiasm which, with its inner drive, impels the individual forward. The passionless person lacks this; for him the principle becomes something external for which he is willing to do both this and that and also the opposite. The life of the passionless person is not a principle that reveals itself and unfolds; on the contrary, his inner life is something quick, continually on the move and chasing after something to do 'for the sake of principle'. Principle in this sense becomes an unnatural something or other, an abstraction just like the public. And although the public is a something so monstrous that even all nations assembled at one time, and even all souls in eternity, are not so numerous as the public, yet everyone including the drunken sailor has a public – and that is also how it is with principle. It is some monstrous something or other from which even the most insignificant person can tease out a most insignificant action and think himself immensely important. A harmless nobody suddenly becomes a hero 'for the sake of principle', and the effect of the situation is basically just as comical as if a man – or everyone, if it became the fashion – were to go about wearing a cap with a sixty-foot peak. If a man 'for the sake of principle' were to have a little button sewn on the breast pocket of his coat, that trivial and perfectly reasonable precaution would suddenly acquire tremendous importance

– not improbably, a society would be founded on the strength of it.

Again, precisely this 'for the sake of principle' nullifies a passionate distinction of decorum; for decorum, as was indicated earlier, is rooted in immediacy (the first or the achieved), in feeling, in inspiration's inner drive and in inner self-consistency. For the sake of principle one can do anything and everything and it essentially makes no difference, just as one's life remains insignificant even if for the sake of principle one supports everything called 'the demand of the times'; even if as a stage extra one becomes just as well known in this guise of *Träger der öffentlichen Meinung*[39] as those barrel-organ figures that appear with the bowl and bow. For the sake of principle one can do anything, take part in anything, and be oneself an inhuman neither one thing nor the other. A man can be interested for the sake of principle in establishing a brothel (indeed, many political observations to this effect have been made by the police), and the same man can for the sake of principle be interested in a new hymnal which the times are supposed to demand. And just as it would be unfair to conclude from the first that the man was dissolute, so might it be overhasty to conclude from the latter that he wanted to read or sing from the hymn-book. In this way everything becomes permissible for the sake of principle; and just as the police 'in the line of duty' enter many places where others are not admitted, and just as one cannot conclude from their presence there anything about a policeman's person, so too can one do everything on principle and evade all personal responsibility. 'For the sake of principle' one tears down what one admires* – which is nonsense, for any bringing forth, any creating, is always latently polemical, because it needs room; but that which pulls down is indeed nothing, and a principle of demolition is emptiness – what does it need room for? But modesty or regret or responsibility have a harder time getting a grip on such behaviour, for after all, it was done for the sake of principle.

What is *superficiality* and its characteristic propensity, 'the urge to show off'? Superficiality is the repealed passionate distinction between

---

* This very example is discussed in the novel, where one of the participants in the conversation calls such conduct 'false to mine and yours [*Falsk i Mit og Dit; Mit og Dit* is also an expression meaning the right of property, trans.]'.

hiddenness and revelation. It is a revelation of emptiness, which in scope does have the trickster's deceptive advantage over essential revelation and its essential homogeneity of depth; superficiality offers a multifarious or omnifarious appearance. And the show-off tendency is the self-infatuation of a conceited reflection. The concealment of the inner life is given no time for anything essential to be deposited that can become revealed, but is much too quickly muddied up; and by way of compensation selfish reflection tries its best to draw all eyes towards this motley show, as does the commercial counsellor's consort, Mrs Waller.

What is *flirtation*? It is the annulled passionate distinction between essentially loving and being essentially dissolute. Neither the essential lover nor the essential debauchee is guilty of flirting, which only trifles with possibility. Thus flirtation is the indulgence to dare brush with evil and a dispensation from realizing the good. Acting for the sake of principle is therefore also to flirt, because it contorts moral action into an abstraction. But flirtation has the advantage in scope, for one can flirt with all sorts of things while only one girl can be loved essentially; and, if understood in the proper erotic sense (even if desire in the time of moral lapse blinds the fickle person), all adding is a subtracting, and the more one adds the more one subtracts.

What does it mean to *reason things out*? It is the repealed passionate disjunction between subjectivity and objectivity. As abstract thought, reasoning is not deep enough dialectically; as belief and conviction, it lacks full-blooded individuality. But reasoning does have the spurious advantage when it comes to scope, for a thinker can comprehend his field of knowledge, a man can have an opinion about something pertaining to a particular discipline, hold a conviction on the strength of a particular life-view, but the person who reasons things out can reason about all things possible.

Anonymity has, in our time, a far more pregnant significance than is perhaps realized; it has almost epigrammatic significance. Not only do people write anonymously, they write anonymously in their own name, indeed speak anonymously. Just as an author puts his whole soul into his style, so a person essentially puts his personality into his speech, though this must be understood with the limiting exception pointed out by Claudius in a similar situation when he said that when you charm a book the spirit emerges — unless there is no spirit there.[40] Nowadays it is possible actually to be speaking with people, and to be forced to admit that what they say is exceedingly sensible, and yet the conversation leaves the impression that one has been speaking with an anonym. The same person can say the most contradictory things, can coolly utter something that, coming from him, is the most bitter satire upon his own life. The remark itself is very sensible, would go over very well at a stockholders' meeting as part of a discussion fabricating some resolution – much as, in an actual factory, paper is made out of rags. But the sum-total of all these many remarks does not amount to personal human discourse such as can be carried on by even the most simple-minded man able to talk of very little but who nevertheless does speak.

The commercial counsellor's consort Mrs Waller's comment on the demonic is very true, and yet as she says it she gives one precisely the impression of being an anonymity, a barrel-organ, a musical box. The remarks become so objective, their range so all-encompassing, that in the end it is altogether incidental who says it, which in terms of speaking humanly corresponds exactly to acting for the sake of principle. And just as the public is a pure abstraction, so in the end will it be with human speech — there will no longer be someone speaking but an objective reflection will gradually impart an atmospheric something, an abstract sound that will render human speech redundant, just as machines make workers redundant. In Germany there are even manuals for lovers, so it will probably end with lovers sitting and speaking anonymously to each other. There are manuals on everything, and being educated will in general soon consist in being word-perfect in a greater or smaller compilation of observations from such manuals, excellence being measured by one's skill in picking out the particular one, just as the compositor picks out letters.

The present age is thus essentially sensible. Perhaps it knows more on average than any previous generation; but it is devoid of passion.*

* For example, even Arnold [the law student, referred to on p. 25 – *trans.*] is far from being dense; on the contrary he is intelligent, but in the way of an aimless person with nothing to engage him completely, who is therefore witty out of boredom, insolent in his despair at being unable to be witty, and smug in his despair at being unable to impress with his insolence.

Everyone is well informed; we all know what path to take, and what paths can be taken, but no one will take them. If someone eventually overcame his reflection and acted, a thousand reflections from outside would immediately form an opposition to him, because only proposals further to consider the matter are received with a surge of enthusiasm, while proposals for action are received with lethargy. Some in their superior smugness would find the enthusiasm of those who act ridiculous; others would be envious because it was the other who made the start when they *knew* just as well as he what was to be done but hadn't done it. Others would exploit the fact that at least one person had acted as an occasion for parading a host of critical observations and fetching out a stock of arguments to show how much more sensibly he *could* have acted. Others would be busy guessing the outcome, and if possible influencing the enterprise in the direction of their own hypotheses. There is a story about two English lords who came riding along and met a luckless horseman about to fall from his horse, which had suddenly started to gallop off while he was shouting for help. One lord glanced at the other and said, 'A hundred guineas he falls off.' 'Taken,' replied the other. They set their thoroughbreds off at a gallop and hurried ahead to get all the gates opened and all obstacles out of the way.

Similarly, the sensibleness of the present age, only with less of the impetuous millionaire heroics, could be personified as someone who, inquisitive, courteous and worldly-wise, would have the passion at most to make a bet. Life's existential tasks have lost the interest of actuality; no illusion protects the divine growth of inwardness that matures to decisions. One person is curious about another, all wait in indecision and versed in evasion for someone to come along who wills something – so as to place their bets on him. And since in this age, in which so little is actually done, such an extraordinary amount occurs in the way of prophecies, apocalypses, hints and insights into the future, there is probably nothing for it but to join in, although I do have the advantage over the others, with their heavy responsibilities in prophesying and warning, in the free and easy certainty that no one will dream of believing me. Therefore I do not even simply ask people to mark an X on the calendar, or go to the trouble of noting whether it comes true or not. For if it does come true, they will have other things to think about than my fortuity, and if it doesn't – well then, I will still be a prophet in the modern sense, for a modern prophet is someone who makes prophecies, nothing more. And that is understand-able, for in a way a prophet can do no more anyway. It was after all Guidance that made the fulfilment tally with the ancient prophet's pronouncements; perhaps we modern prophets, lacking Guidance's endorsement, could add, as Thales did, 'What we prophesy will either happen or not happen, for the gift of prophecy is one that the gods have bestowed also upon us.'[41]

It is so far from the truth that the age will be saved by the idea of sociality, of communion, that this idea constitutes, on the contrary, the scepticism needed for the development of individuality properly to occur, in so far as every individual either is lost or, disciplined by abstraction, finds himself religiously. The principle of association (which can at best have validity with respect to material interests) is, in our time, not affirmative but negative; it is an evasion, a diversion, an illusion, whose dialectic is this: as this principle strengthens individuals, it also enervates them; through solidarity it strengthens numerically, but this from the ethical point of view is also to debilitate. Only when the single individual has acquired in himself an ethical stance in face of the whole world can there be any question of genuinely uniting; otherwise, the union of the individually weak becomes just about as uncomely and corrupt as child marriages. Formerly, the ruler, the man of excellence, those of rank, each had his own opinion; the others had the closedness or inflexibility of not daring or of not being able to have an opinion. Now everyone can have an opinion but, in having it, they have to join forces numerically. Twenty-five signatures to the silliest notion is an opinion, the most eminent mind's most well-considered opinion is a paradox. Public opinion is an inorganic something or other, an abstraction. When the context has become meaningless large surveys are useless; the best thing to do then is pick out the discourse's individual parts. When the mouth gossips there is no point in wanting to say something coherent; the best thing to do is take each word by itself – similarly, with the situation of individuals.

The change-over will also be this: whereas in older formations (of relations between generation and individual) the non-commissioned officers, officers, company commanders, generals, the hero (that is, the men of excellence, the men of rank within their various hierarchies, the leaders), were *recognizable*, and each (according to his authority) along with his little detachment was picturesquely and organically ordered within the whole, each supported by and supporting the whole, now the men of excellence, the leaders (according to their respective rank) will be without authority precisely because they will have divinely understood the diabolical principle of levelling; they will be *unrecogniz-able*, like plainclothes police carrying their badge secretly and giving support only negatively – that is, by repulsion – while the infinite impartiality of abstraction judges every individual, examines him in his isolation.

This formation is dialectically the opposite of that of the judges and prophets, and just as the danger for them was that of not being respected for their respective authorities, so the danger for the unrecognizables is to be recognized, to be lured into acquiring respect and status as authorities, thus preventing the highest development. For they are unrecognizable, or like secret agents, not according to a private instruction from God – for that is the situation of the prophets and judges – but they are unrecognizable (without authority) because they have themselves apprehended the universal in equality before God, and because they apprehend this every moment, answerably, something which prevents them from being distracted and becoming guilty of acting inconsistently with the requirements of their life-view. This formation is dialectically the opposite of the systematizing that makes the generation anticipated in the men of excellence the supporting factor for individuals, since as an abstraction, negatively supported by the unrecognizables, it turns now polemically against individuals – so as to save every single individual religiously.

And thus, when the generation which has itself wanted to level, has wanted to be emancipated and to revolt, has wanted to do away with authority and has thereby in the scepticism of association brought about the desolating forest fire of abstraction; when this generation, by levelling through the scepticism of association, has done away with individual personalities and all the organic concretions, has got humanity in their place and made man's relation to man a matter of numerical ratios; and when for a moment this generation has thus found diversion in the broad vista of an abstract infinity, undisturbed by the limitation of even the slightest elevation; when there is 'only air and sea'[42] – then begins the work in which individuals must help themselves, each on his own. For it will not be as it once was, that when things began to get a little hazy for them, individuals could look to the nearest eminence to regain their bearings. That time is now past; they must either be lost in the dizziness of abstract infinity or be infinitely saved in the essentiality of religiousness.

Very many may cry out in despair, but that will not help, it is now too late. If authority and power have formerly been misused in the world and have brought a nemesis of revolution upon themselves, then it was in fact impotence and weakness that had aspired to stand on their own feet and that have therefore now brought that nemesis upon themselves. And not one of the unrecognizables dare presume to help directly, to speak directly, to teach directly, to make the decision at the head of the crowd (instead of helping the individual towards the decision, where he himself is, supporting him negatively). That would mean that unrecognizable's dismissal, because he would be meddling in the short-sighted inventiveness of human sympathy instead of obeying the orders of the deity, the deity so wrathful yet so full of grace; for development is still a step forward, because all those individuals who are saved gain the specific gravity of religiousness, gain its essentiality at first hand from God. Then it will be said, 'Look, all is ready;[43] look, the cruelty of abstraction reveals the vanity of the finite as such; look, the abyss of the infinite is opening up; look, the sharp scythe of levelling lets all, each for himself, leap over the blade – look, God waits! Leap, then, into the embrace of God.' But even the most trusted of the unrecognizables, whether it was the woman who carried him in her belly he would help, or the girl for whom he would gladly give his life, shall not dare, and could not, help them – they must make the leap by themselves, and God's infinite love is not a relation at second hand for them. Yet the unrecognizables (according to their respective ranks) will have a twofold task compared with the men of distinction (in the same ranks) in an earlier formation, for the unrecognizables have to keep on working – and at the same time strive to conceal the fact that they are still working.

But the desolating abstraction of levelling will be continually kept going by its servants, in case it should end with an earlier formation's return. These servants of levelling are the servants of the power of evil, for levelling itself is not of the deity, and every good human being will have moments when he could weep over its desolateness; but the deity permits levelling and wants to cooperate with the individuals, that is, each for himself, and to bring out the most high. The unrecognizables recognize the servants of levelling but dare not use power or authority against them, for then things would regress, because it would be instantly obvious to a third party that the unrecognizable was an authority, and then this third party would be kept from the most high. Only through a *suffering* act will the unrecognizable dare help levelling along, and will by that same suffering act condemn the tool. He dare not defeat the levelling directly – that would mean his dismissal, since his action would suggest authority – but he will defeat it in suffering, and express again thereby the law of his existence, which is not to rule, guide, lead, but in suffering to serve, to help indirectly. Those who have not made the leap would interpret the suffering act of the unrecognizable as his defeat, and those who have made the leap would have a notion that it was his victory; but there would be no certainty because certainty could come only from him, and for him to give certainty to one single man would mean his certain dismissal, for he would have been unfaithful to the deity and playing at authority – he would not in obeying the deity have learned to love men infinitely by constraining himself, but fraudulently, by domineeringly constraining them, even if they asked for it.

But I break off here. Naturally the only interest this can have is as a prank, for if it is true that every person is to work out his own salvation, then making prophecies about the world's future is tolerable and admissible at best as a form of recreation, a joke, just like playing bowls or tilting at the barrel.

My thoughts, which have not for a moment forgotten *Two Ages*, turn back to it in grateful conclusion. The criticism I have contributed is what I have learned from the author's novel, and *this is understood in the sense that, if there is anything immature, untrue or foolish in my presentation, then that is my own doing*. Anyone who finds it false should therefore look to me, but anyone who finds truth in what I have said, finds his view of life strengthened or enriched by it, is referred to the teacher – the novel's author.

As little in the critique as in the novel has the question been one of judging or evaluating the ages – only of depicting them. The novel's Preface explicitly points out that both approaches could be equally valid, and the novel ends with the hope for the present age expressed by the present age; which is, no doubt, as was said before, on average far more intelligent, informed and reflectively developed than was the age of revolution; and when it gets the strength it will act with far greater intensity in relation to the extensity at its disposal. For the present age admittedly has the advantage in scope but not in intensity, which is why it is true of the present age as in the novel that our men of excellence belong to an older generation,* while among the younger ones there is more general competence but no eminence. If power and enthusiasm take over in individuals, it may become evident that really the present age stands, or has been standing, in its own light. Just as a woman when she puts on far too much finery fails to look chic because that requires tasteful proportion, so the present age seems to have decked itself out too much in the multifariousness of reflection to give harmonious balance a chance. But one must always bear in mind that reflection in, or by, itself is not something pernicious, that on the contrary its thorough working through is the condition of more intensive action.

The conditions for inspired action are these: first comes the immediate inspiration; then the time for prudence, which because immediate inspiration calculates nothing, by virtue of its calculating ingenuity takes on an appearance of superiority; and then finally, the strongest and most intensive enthusiasm, which, following upon prudence, therefore sees what the most prudent thing to do is, but disdains to do it, and for that very reason acquires the intensity of infinite enthusiasm. This most

---

* If I may be allowed to allude in a note to an earlier statement concerning the older generation: 'it is still unmistakably represented in not a few significant venerable individualities'. See *Af en endnu Levendes Papirer* [*From the Papers of One Still Living*, *Søren Kierkegaards Skrifter* (Gads Forlag, Copenhagen, 1997), vol. 1, pp. 22–3].

intensive enthusiasm will for the time being be completely misunder-
stood, and the question is whether it can ever be popular – that is,
whether prudence will ever be so much a presupposition in the average
man as to lose, in his eyes, its seductive charm, so that he will not only
be able to be equal to it but also in the most intensive enthusiasm, so
to speak, waste it, content with the satisfaction of infinite enthusiasm;
for just because it goes against prudence, action arising from such
enthusiasm will never be obvious.

Thus Socrates was no man of immediate enthusiasm; on the contrary,
he was prudent enough to see what he should do to be acquitted, but
he disdained to act accordingly, just as he refused the speech offered to
him.[44] For that reason alone there is nothing obvious about his heroic
death; even in death he continues to be ironical by posing to all wise
people the problem of whether he really had been all that wise, seeing
that he did the opposite. It is on this point that prudence gets caught in
the verdict of its own, and of the surroundings', reflection. It fears that
acting contrary to prudence will be confused with acting without
prudence. This danger is unknown to immediate inspiration, which is
why the impetus of the most high is needed in order to break through.
And this most intensive enthusiasm for the most high is not some
rhetorical poppycock about a higher and still higher and a highest-of-all;
it is recognizable by its category, that it acts against the understanding.
Thus immediate good-naturedness knows nothing of the danger of
reflection either, whereby a good nature could be confused with weakness – for which very reason a religious impetus has to follow reflection
in order to set good nature afloat.

On first reading *Two Ages*, I thought it might have been more fitting
for the author to give it another title, more in the spirit of *A Story of
Everyday Life*, because the reflection of the age didn't properly become
clear to me in the presentation. Later I became convinced of the
opposite, and have had both a rich and, for me, most welcome opportunity to admire the author's ingenuity. Thus my position cannot be that
of a hard-pressed critic who, after hastily leafing through the book, in
a fit of good humour seizes his pen to draw others' attention to the
work. On the contrary, I have read the novel through several times,
and wish that the esteemed unknown author would regard this perhaps

excessively lengthy review as a token of my acknowledgement of the pleasure I have had in reading it, and of my having found it to accc with the memory of so many an earlier pleasure for which I am indebted to this signature. For me, at least – and I really believe this must be true for anyone who has learned to look humanly at life – the signature's twenty years are not something that disturbs or secretly tickles an impatient curiosity for novelty – rather, they constitute something that increases our pleasure. A capital stock, as we know, doubles in twenty years. Shouldn't the human powers of appreciation similarly increase? If so, pleasure experienced in *A Story of Everyday Life* and appreciation of its author should also have doubled. And so, too, will it be with a *human being*'s ability to appreciate, unless he inhumanly confuses himself with some abstract something or other – with the age, our age, etc. – and, rather, by himself fully grasps what it is to be a human being, finding his joy in excellence increasing with each year that passes, and thereby finding again the edification to live in appreciation of his elders.

Directing attention to the novel is not my business, and would seem to me improperly presumptuous. But if anyone were to seek my advice, I would counsel them to read it, and if they have already read it, to read it again.

NOTES

Dedication

1. *unnamed yet so famed*: The original text plays on the pair *navnløs* (nameless, anonymous) and *navnkundig* (celebrated, but in the sense of a famous name, as in the French *renommé*).

Preface

1. *Nordisk Literaturtidende*: A journal of current Scandinavian literature edited by J. F. Giødwad and P. D. Ploug, editors of the Copenhagen newspaper *Fædrelandet* (*The Fatherland*).

Introduction

1. *'a wandering star'*: Jude 13: '. . . wandering stars, to whom is reserved the blackness of darkness for ever.'

2. *like that new pharaoh* . . . : Exodus 1:8: 'Now there arose up a new king over Egypt, which knew not Joseph.'

3. *eo ipso*: 'By virtue of that very fact.'

4. *Elagabalus*: Roman Emperor, AD 218–22, under the self-given name M. Aurelius Antoninus, also called Heliogabalus, having as a child been made priest of the Sun-god of that name. Stupid and vain, he was killed by his own soldiers at the age of seventeen.

5. *that the judgement he pronounces* . . . : Matthew 7:1–2: 'Judge not, that ye be not judged. For with what judgment ye judge, ye shall be judged: and with what measure ye mete, it shall be measured to you again.' Cf. Mark 4:24.

6. *Slow to listen, quick to judge*: James 1:19: '. . . let every man be swift to hear, slow to speak, slow to wrath.'

7. *the Socratic teaching* . . . : Cf. Diogenes Laertius (II 22), according to whom

Socrates said of Heraclitus' words that since what he understood was good he presumed what he did not understand was also good.

8. *the consequent following that brilliant antecedent*: 'Antecedent' and 'consequent' are terms used to refer to the parts of a hypothetical proposition, the antecedent beginning 'If . . .' and the consequent beginning 'then . . .'.

9. *One cannot call it beginning with nothing*: That philosophy should and could begin with no presuppositions was familiar to the many versed in Hegel's philosophy at the time.

10. *'the demand of the age'*: An expression made popular by J. L. Heiberg, Madame Gyllembourg's son. See Translator's Introduction. That it was the age itself that made demands, rather than individuals who made demands of themselves independently of the age, was an idea constantly ridiculed by Kierkegaard.

11. *the Ancient of Days*: Daniel 7:13: 'I saw in the night visions, and, behold, one like the Son of man came with the clouds of heaven, and came to the Ancient of days, and they brought him near before him.' For St John's similar vision, see Revelation 1:7.

12. *'one in all'*: Title of one of the feuilleton stories comprising *A Story of Everyday Life*. See Translator's Introduction.

13. *'moderation be known unto all men'*: Philippians 4:5.

14. *faithful over only a few things*: Matthew 25:21: 'His lord said unto him, Well done, thou good and faithful servant: thou hast been faithful over a few things.'

15. *stricte sic dicta*: 'Strictly speaking.'

16. *ideality*: In distinguishing 'ideality' from 'reality', the philosophies of the time marked off an area we might today refer to in terms of 'concepts' or 'conceptual schemes' as distinct from mere things. At that time the former were more closely linked to possibilities of fulfilling action than today, closing the gap that has now grown in our language between 'idea' and 'ideal'. It is the latter that is implied by talking of religion's ideality.

17. *the peace and incorruptibility of a quiet spirit*: I Peter 3:4: 'But let it be the hidden man of the heart, in that which is not corruptible, even the ornament of a meek and quiet spirit, which is in the sight of God of great price.'

18. *Professor Heiberg*: Johan Ludvig Heiberg, son of the author of *Two Ages*. See Translator's Introduction.

19. *For whatever objections there are . . .* : Under the pseudonym Nicolaus Notabene (in *Forord* (*Prefaces*, C. A. Reitzel, Copenhagen, 1844); in *Søren Kierkegaards Skrifter* (*SKS*, Gads Forlag, Copenhagen, 1997), vol. 4, pp. 463–527) Kierkegaard had castigated Danish writers, including Madame Gyllembourg's son, for indulging in this seasonal marketing practice.

20. *a resting place or . . . a place of prayer*: The Danish *Bedested* can mean a place of prayer and a place for travellers to rest.

21. *cito citissime*: 'With all possible haste.' The Latin was once written on letters intended for express delivery.

22. *those novellas*: The short stories that went under the name of *A Story of Everyday Life*. See Translator's Introduction.

1 Prospectus of the Contents of Both Parts

1. *Waller*: in *Two Ages* spelled 'Valler'.

2. *'whom the hard times have made prematurely hard to please'*: A conflation of two passages from *Two Ages*, p. 8; Kierkegaard's pagination in the text following refers to the first edition (J. L. Heiberg, Copenhagen, 1845).

3. *Madame W.*: Waller's wife has the title 'Madame', while in Part Two the wife of Waller's son, Commercial Counsellor Waller, is called 'Mrs Waller' though also *Commerceraadinden*, which may be roughly translated 'the commercial counsellor's consort'. At that time 'Madame' was a title generally applied to the wives of men of fairly good standing, such as Merchant Waller; while 'Mrs' (*Fru*) and the *-inde* ending gave higher status and were accorded to wives of men in state office. A *Frue* was a 'lady'. Later in the century both forms of address lost their standing. 'Madame' was applied especially (originally ironically) to proletarian wives, while almost every middle-class married woman became a *Frue* or 'Mrs'.

4. *'qui ne revient plus pour les amants . . .'*: From a song by the French writer Jean-Pierre Claris de Florian (1755–94), quoted in *Two Ages*, p. 171.

5. *'where for ten summers now . . .'*: A modified quotation from *Two Ages*, p. 177.

6. *'Maren'*: Not a normal abbreviation for 'Mariane'; in Danish *Mare* means 'nightmare' and *Maren* 'the nightmare'.

7. *'advocate for a vanished age – or against a present one'*: *Two Ages*, pp. 231–2.

8. *twenty-five rix-dollars*: A rix-dollar (*rixstaler* or *riksdaler*) was a coin minted the year the Danish State Bank (Riksbank) declared bankruptcy (1813, the year of Kierkegaard's birth), to stay the monetary chaos that arose following the bombardment of Copenhagen by the British Navy in September 1807. Besides the attack itself, and the damage it caused, the continuing alliance with Napoleon proved equally costly for Denmark. It was not until the early 1830s that the country began to show significant signs of recovery. A rix-dollar at this time was worth between three and four crowns, equivalent in value to over four pounds sterling or five to six US dollars today.

9. *'Amen, yes, we would hope for that'*: *Two Ages*, p. 285.

II An Aesthetic Reading of the Novel and Its Details

1. *'heart pounded violently, more violently than the Corybants'* . . .': Plato, *Symposium* 215e. Corybants were priests of Cybele or Rhea in Phrygia, who celebrated her worship with ecstatic dances.

2. *'looks like someone pestered* . . .': *Two Ages*, p. 188.

3. *'Those are slanderous words you are using'*: *Two Ages*, pp. 9–10.

4. *'for all the blessings she enjoys in this dear household'*: *Two Ages*, p. 25.

5. *that winged steed*: Pegasus, the winged horse of the fountain that sprang from the blood of Medusa when Perseus struck off her head. After several escapades, Pegasus continued his ascent to heaven and dwelt among the stars.

6. *the great poet's*: Adam G. Oehlenschläger (1779–1850), the Danish poet and dramatist. (See *Oehlenschlägers Tragødier* (Copenhagen, 1841–4), III, pp. 136f.)

7. *'my little wife'*: *Two Ages*, p. 64.

8. *the middle term*: In classical syllogistic logic, the term that appears in both premises (Every *man* is mortal, Socrates is a *man*) but not in the conclusion (Socrates is mortal). In Kierkegaard's time 'middle term' had acquired a wider application through Hegel, designating that by which two apparently opposite notions must be 'mediated' in order to apply to one and the same reality. Here Kierkegaard's use is informal and indeed metaphorical.

9. *a comparison of the two ages*: The author of *Two Ages* quotes Prosper Mérimée's *Chronique du temps de Charles IX* in the Preface and adds: 'These observations on the relation of the present age to a not so distant past seem to be still more relevant if the discussion is about much closer periods of world-historical significance.'

10. *a 'little slut' like that, as her stepmother calls her*: *Two Ages*, p. 223.

11. *an ancient author*: Ammianus Marcellinus (born Greek, last of the great Roman historians, of whose writings eighteen books of his history of the Roman empire are extant), XXIII 6, 85–6.

12. *'Neither will I give back yours* . . .': *Two Ages*, pp. 222–3.

13. *'by the quiet virtues'*: A rendition of the author's version in *Two Ages*, p. 217.

14. *'You too, Brutus, my son!'*: Tranquillus Suetonius (Roman historian who wrote *Lives of the Caesars*), *Caesar* 82.

15. *ecclesia pressa*: A suppressed and therefore hidden church.

16. *the consequent*: See note 8, p. 104.

17. *referre pedem*: 'Retreat.'

18. *purity of heart is to will one thing*: James 4:8: 'Cleanse your hands, ye sinners; and purify your hearts, ye double minded.' In March the following year (1847) Kierkegaard published three *Opbyggelige Taler i forekjellig Aand* (*Edifying*

Discourses in a Different Tenor, C. A. Reitzel, Copenhagen, 1847), the first of them on the proposition that 'purity of heart is to will one thing'. This was written in 1846 subsequent to publication of the *Review*.

19. *omnia ad conscientiam, nil ad ostentationem*: Pliny the Younger, I 22, 5: 'All things according to conscience, not to appearance.'

20. *valore intrinseco*: 'According to the intrinsic value.'

21. *true to the category*: This probably means 'true to the category of its framework', namely human psychology.

22. *something extinct and ruined* . . . : *Two Ages*, pp. 181–2, where Milner uses these expressions of the lands (Greek, Oriental and American) that Lusard has visited.

23. *Just a single line of Lusard's* . . . : Kierkegaard gives a reference (p. 243) in the margin which could be to Mrs Waller's dismissive remark on Henrik Hertz's drama *Svanehammen* (*Swan's Wings*, lit. 'Swan's Skin'): 'It proves that the author must himself be too much of a swan to swim in a village pond.' Hertz (1798–1870) was a Danish poet of Jewish descent.

III The Results of Observing the Two Ages

1. *The naked Archimedes* . . . : According to the story he jumped naked from the bath when he discovered the principle of specific gravity and ran into the street crying, 'I've found it [*Eureka*]!'

2. *Agrippa*: See Acts 26:27–9: 'King Agrippa, believest thou the prophets? I know that thou believest. Then Agrippa said unto Paul, Almost thou persuadest me to be a Christian. And Paul said, I would to God, that not only thou, but also all that hear me this day, were both almost, and altogether such as I am, except these bonds.'

3. *plerophoria eis pathos*: 'Fullness of pathos.'

4. *the children's crusade*: A movement in 1212 of thousands of children from Germany and France aiming to reach the Holy Land and recapture Jerusalem from the Turks. None reached that destination, those sold to slavery in North Africa coming nearest.

5. *takes a wrong turn* . . . : The Danish exploits the pun in the expression *farer vild* ('goes astray') and *farer ilde* ('goes badly with').

6. *evasion*: The original exploits the parallel between *Udsigt* ('prospect') and *Udflugt* ('evasion').

7. *Vis inertia*: 'Inertial force.'

8. *tergiversation*: 'Turning one's back' or 'prevarication'.

9. *the encyclopédistes*: Encyclopedias, as comprehensive reference works, date from classical times, but the most dedicated and notable encyclopedists appeared in eighteenth-century Britain and France in connection with the Enlightenment. The 35-volume *Encyclopédie* of Denis Diderot (1713–84) and his associates (1751–76) became exemplary.

10. *A profound religious renunciation* . . . : I John 2:15: 'Love not the world, neither the things that are in the world. If any man love the world, the love of the Father is not in him.'

11. *mir nichts und dir nichts*: 'Without so much as a take your leave.'

12. *knight of faith*: A key figure in *Fear and Trembling*, trans. Alastair Hannay (Penguin Books, Harmondsworth, 1985).

13. *dare to say 'Tomorrow'* . . . : James 4:14–15: 'Whereas ye know not what shall be on the morrow. For what is your life? It is even a vapour, that appeareth for a little time, and then vanisheth away. For that ye ought to say, If the Lord will . . .'

14. *carefree as the lily of the field* . . . : Matthew 6:28–9: 'And why take ye thought for raiment? Consider the lilies of the field, how they grow; they toil not, neither do they spin. And yet I say unto you, That even Solomon in all his glory was not arrayed like one of these.'

15. *ab posse ad esse*: 'From possibility to actuality.'

16. *like all knowledge, reflection too increases sorrow*: Ecclesiastes 1:18: 'For in much wisdom is much grief: and he that increaseth knowledge increaseth sorrow.'

17. *facticity*: Refers to the unalterable context of life, what remains the same through change, and what one can ignore only in forgetfulness or flights of imagination. In twentieth-century philosophy the term has acquired a more technical sense, referring to those structural aspects of life that we do not easily discern but which govern our thought and action. Kierkegaard's concern was to remind philosophers of the need to apply their thought to 'concrete' reality.

18. *charasso*: Inf. *charassein*, Greek, meaning 'make pointed', 'sharpen', also 'engrave'. 'Character' is from the same root: an engraved mark or sign, a letter.

19. *sorites*: Lit. 'heap', a compound syllogism or chain of syllogisms in which the conclusion of each prosyllogism is omitted. The metaphor conveys the idea of a procedure going on that will produce something on its own.

20. *'in each other's mouth'*: Kierkegaard alludes to an expression literally translatable as 'talking in each other's mouth', or 'talking to each other at the same time'.

21. *the grand master himself* . . . : Socrates.

22. *bearing witness with their spirit*: Romans 8:16: 'The Spirit itself beareth witness with our spirit, that we are the children of God.'

23. *vitia splendida*: 'Glittering vices.'

24. *the diagonal in a parallelogram of forces*: In dynamics, the resultant of two forces

acting at one point, if represented in quantity and direction by two sides of a parallelogram, is similarly represented by the diagonal drawn from the same point.

25. *they know not what they do*: Luke 23:34: 'Then said Jesus, Father, forgive them; for they know not what they do. And they parted his raiment, and cast lots.'

26. *examen rigorosum*: 'Rigorous examination' or 'trial' for higher qualification.

27. *evil*: Genesis 50:20: '. . . ye thought evil against me; but God meant it unto good, to bring to pass, as it is this day, to save much people alive.'

28. *just as offence must needs come* . . . : Luke 17:1: 'Then said he unto the disciples, It is impossible but that offences will come: but woe unto him, through whom they come!'

29. *Holger Danske*: A hero of Danish legend first immortalized in a French medieval poem (*Ogier de Danemarche*). First written in French, it was translated into Latin, then later into Danish by Christen (Christiern) Pedersen (*c.* 1480–1554), who lived for several years in Paris.

30. *a peep-show*: A reference to the contemporary Danish poet and aesthetician Henrik Hertz's *Perspektivkassen* (*Peep-Show*).

31. *in partibus infidelium*: 'In non-Catholic countries.'

32. *Weep not for him, but weep for yourselves*: Luke 23:28: 'But Jesus turning unto them said, Daughters of Jerusalem, weep not for me, but weep for yourselves, and for your children.'

33. *just as that resolute number three* . . . : Plato, *Phaedo* 104c.

34. *time both to speak and stay silent*: Ecclesiastes 3:7: '. . . a time to keep silence, and a time to speak.'

35. *ideality*: See note 16, p. 104.

36. *aduton*: 'Inner sanctum.'

37. *Link*: A character in J. L. Heiberg's *Nej* (*No*).

38. *posito*: 'Supposition' or 'posit'.

39. *Träger der öffentlichen Meinung*: 'Bearer of public opinion.'

40. *pointed out by Claudius* . . . : A reference to Matthias Claudius (1740–1815), a German poet born in Holstein who wrote under the name 'Asmus'. Kierkegaard possessed his collected works, which appeared under the title *Asmus omnia sua secum portans* (*Asmus Carries All His Things with Him*).

41. *'What we prophesy will either happen* . . .': Horace, *Satires* II, 5, 59, s. It was said by Tiresias, not by the pre-Socratic philosopher.

42. *'only air and sea'*: Calling to mind a caravaner's song in Oehlenschläger's *Aladdin*, Act 5, *Digterværker* (*Literary Works*), I–XVIII (Copenhagen, 1844–9), VI, p. 234.

43. *'Look, all is ready'*: Luke 14:17: 'And sent his servant at supper time to say to them that were bidden, Come; for all things are now ready.' The rich man had prepared a dinner but those he invited all excused themselves, whereupon he told his servant to fetch the poor, the maimed, the halt and the blind instead.

44. *Thus Socrates* . . . : Diogenes Laertius II, 40.

READ MORE IN PENGUIN

In every corner of the world, on every subject under the sun, Penguin represents quality and variety – the very best in publishing today.

For complete information about books available from Penguin – including Puffins, Penguin Classics and Arkana – and how to order them, write to us at the appropriate address below. Please note that for copyright reasons the selection of books varies from country to country.

In the United Kingdom: Please write to *Dept. EP, Penguin Books Ltd, Bath Road, Harmondsworth, West Drayton, Middlesex UB7 0DA*

In the United States: Please write to *Consumer Services, Penguin Putnam Inc., 405 Murray Hill Parkway, East Rutherford, New Jersey 07073-2136.* VISA and MasterCard holders call 1-800-631-8571 to order Penguin titles

In Canada: Please write to *Penguin Books Canada Ltd, 10 Alcorn Avenue, Suite 300, Toronto, Ontario M4V 3B2*

In Australia: Please write to *Penguin Books Australia Ltd, 487 Maroondah Highway, Ringwood, Victoria 3134*

In New Zealand: Please write to *Penguin Books (NZ) Ltd, Private Bag 102902, North Shore Mail Centre, Auckland 10*

In India: Please write to *Penguin Books India Pvt Ltd, 11 Community Centre, Panchsheel Park, New Delhi 110017*

In the Netherlands: Please write to *Penguin Books Netherlands bv, Postbus 3507, NL-1001 AH Amsterdam*

In Germany: Please write to *Penguin Books Deutschland GmbH, Metzlerstrasse 26, 60594 Frankfurt am Main*

In Spain: Please write to *Penguin Books S. A., Bravo Murillo 19, 1°B, 28015 Madrid*

In Italy: Please write to *Penguin Italia s.r.l., Via Vittorio Emanuele 45/a, 20094 Corsico, Milano*

In France: Please write to *Penguin France, 12, Rue Prosper Ferradou, 31700 Blagnac*

In Japan: Please write to *Penguin Books Japan Ltd, Iidabashi KM-Bldg, 2-23-9 Koraku, Bunkyo-Ku, Tokyo 112-0004*

In South Africa: Please write to *Penguin Books South Africa (Pty) Ltd, P.O. Box 751093, Gardenview, 2047 Johannesburg*

READ MORE IN PENGUIN

A CHOICE OF CLASSICS

Jacob Burckhardt	**The Civilization of the Renaissance in Italy**
Carl von Clausewitz	**On War**
Meister Eckhart	**Selected Writings**
Friedrich Engels	**The Origin of the Family**
	The Condition of the Working Class in England
Goethe	**Elective Affinities**
	Faust Parts One and Two (in two volumes)
	Italian Journey
	Maxims and Reflections
	Selected Verse
	The Sorrows of Young Werther
Jacob and Wilhelm Grimm	**Selected Tales**
E. T. A. Hoffmann	**Tales of Hoffmann**
Friedrich Hölderlin	**Selected Poems and Fragments**
Henrik Ibsen	**Brand**
	A Doll's House and Other Plays
	Ghosts and Other Plays
	Hedda Gabler and Other Plays
	The Master Builder and Other Plays
	Peer Gynt
Søren Kierkegaard	**Fear and Trembling**
	Papers and Journals
	The Sickness Unto Death
Georg Christoph Lichtenberg	**Aphorisms**
Karl Marx	**Capital** (in three volumes)
Karl Marx/Friedrich Engels	**The Communist Manifesto**
Friedrich Nietzsche	**The Birth of Tragedy**
	Beyond Good and Evil
	Ecce Homo
	Human, All Too Human
	Thus Spoke Zarathustra
Friedrich Schiller	**Mary Stuart**
	The Robbers/Wallenstein

BY THE SAME AUTHOR

Either/Or: A Fragment of Life
Abridged, translated and with an introdcution and notes by Alastair Hannay

Kierkegaard was one of the most startlingly original thinkers of the nineteenth century. *Either/Or* (1843) is the earliest of his major works.

Sheltering behind the persona of a fictitious editor, Kierkegaard brings together an astonishingly diverse range of material – including reflections on Mozart, a sermon and the famous Seducer's Diary – and asks us to choose between two opposing ways of life. We might, as Alastair Hannay suggests in his penetrating Introduction, view the aesthetic young man in Part One as 'the modern hero, richly egocentric, tragically melancholic'. Judge Vilhelm's defence of romantic love and marriage in Part Two makes him either 'a hopeless bore and hypocrite' or the spokesman for a humanly fulfilling ethical life.

Does Kierkegaard mean us to prefer one of the alternatives? Or are we thrown back on the existentialist idea of radical choice? Many such questions are raised by a text with an almost unparalleled power to stimulate and challenge; this lightly abridged new edition makes it freshly accessible in a single annotated volume.

Fear and Trembling
Translated with an introduction and notes by Alastair Hannay

Abraham's unreserved submission to God's will provides the focus for this religious and ethical polemic. Writing under the pseudonym of *Johannes de silentio*, Kierkegaard uses the form of a dialectical lyric to present his conception of faith. Abraham is portrayed as a great man, who chose to sacrifice his son, Isaac, in the face of conflicting expectations and in defiance of any conceivable ethical standard. The infamous and controversial 'teleological suspension of the ethical' challenged the contemporary views of Hegel's universal moral system, and the suffering individual must alone make a choice 'on the strength of the absurd'.

Kierkegaard's writings have inspired both modern Protestant theology and existentialism, and this edition of *Fear and Trembling* contains a full introduction and notes which complement a key work in the psychology of religious belief.

BY THE SAME AUTHOR

The Sickness unto Death
Translated with an introduction and notes by Alastair Hannay

'The biggest danger, that of losing myself, can pass off in the world as quietly as if it were nothing; every other loss, an arm, a leg, five dollars, a wife, etc., is bound to be noticed'.

So writes Kierkegaard through his pseudonymous persona, Anti-Climacus, in what is one of his greatest works of philosophy. For Anti-Climacus, a committed Christian, the human being's goal is to gain eternal life through direct accountability to God in this life, and to discover true selfhood is to acknowledge that ideal.

The Sickness unto Death is a profound exploration of why, very often, people fail to do this. Digging deep in the graveyard of denial, refusal and despair (both conscious and unconscious), it unearths the concept of absolute individuality and the self-awareness that has as its ideal a paradigm of selflessness.

Papers and Journals: A Selection
Translated with an introduction and notes by Alastair Hannay

In presenting this selection from his papers and journals, Alastair Hannay set out to provide 'as comprehensive a picture of Kierkegaard's life and work as is possible within the confines of a single manageable volume'.

Since Kierkegaard often expressed himself elsewhere through pseudonyms and disguises, it is in these private reflections and reactions to events, literature and the people around him that he reveals most directly his personality and the development of his thought. It is here that we see him living out the conflict which formed the basis for *Either/Or*. It is here that he rejects his father's conventional Christianity and forges the idea of the 'leap of faith'.

A combination of philosophical and theoretical argument, vivid natural description and sharply honed wit, this book clearly reveals Kierkegaard as one of the world's liveliest and most stimulating thinkers. Yet perhaps even more impressive is the scale of his moral achievement, the passionate integrity of his efforts 'to find a truth which is truth *for me*, to find *the idea for which I am willing to live or die*'.